Biblical Framework Counseling
(Basic Training Course)

Dr. Nicolas Ellen

Biblical Framework Counseling
(Basic Training Course)

Copyright © 2008 by Dr. Nicolas Ellen

All rights reserved in all countries. No part of this material may be reproduced, stored in a retrieval system, or transmitted in any form or by any means electronic, mechanical, photocopying, recording, or otherwise without prior written permission of the author, publisher and/or copyright owners, except as provided by USA copyright law.

Readers may order copies by visiting www.mycounselingcorner.com

Published and Printed By Expository Counseling Center
Houston, Texas

Unless otherwise noted, scripture references are taken from the New American Standard Bible. © The Lockman Foundation, 1960, 1962, 1963, 1968, 1971, 1972, 1973, 1975, 1977.

Publisher's Cataloging in Publication

Ellen, Dr. Nicolas: *Biblical Framework Counseling*
1. Counseling 2. Psychology 3. Christianity 4. Discipleship

ISBN 978-0-9779690-7-4

Table of Contents

Course Outline	*5*
Section 1	*9*
Section 2	*19*
Section 3	*29*
Section 4	*41*
Section 5	*51*
Section 6	*65*
Section 7	*73*
Section 8	*85*
Section 9	*83*
Section 10	*101*
Section 11	*109*
Section 12	*117*
Section 13	*121*
Section 14	*125*
Bibliography	*131*

Biblical Framework Counseling
(Basic Training Course)

WEEK ONE	SECTION ONE

- NO STUDENT IS ABOVE HIS TEACHER; WORLD VIEW KEY QUESTIONS
- EVALUATING A COUNSELING MODEL, THREE MAJOR TYPES OF COUNSELING SYSTEMS; WHY PROMOTE BIBLICAL COUNSELING ABOVE OTHER COUNSELING MODELS?
- REASONS WE SHOULD NOT INTEGRATE HUMAN WISDOM WITH THE WORD OF GOD
- REVIEW OF WHY TO PROMOTE BIBLICAL COUNSELING ABOVE OTHER COUNSELING MODELS
- *READ: THE HEART OF MAN AND THE MENTAL DISORDERS(INTRODUCTION)*

WEEK TWO	SECTION TWO

- REASONS WE SHOULD NOT INTEGRATE HUMAN WISDOM WITH THE WORD OF GOD
- THE NATURE OF MAN
- THE CONNECTION OF MAN'S MENTAL SOUNDNESS WITH HIS IMMATERIAL BEING
- THREE KEY RESPONSES TO PEOPLE AND CIRCUMSTANCES
- WHAT I CANNOT AND CAN CONTROL
- WHAT MAN IS RESPONSIBLE FOR BEFORE GOD AND WHAT MAN IS NOT RESPONSIBLE FOR BEFORE GOD
- *READ: THE HEART OF MAN AND THE MENTAL DISORDERS;(THE NATURE OF MAN CH 1)*

WEEK THREE	SECTION THREE

- HOW PEACE, MENTAL SOUNDNESS, AND STABILITY ARE CONNECTED TO YOUR RELATIONSHIP WITH GOD
- THE CENTRALITY OF SALVATION
- THE DANGER OF SPIRITUAL AMNESIA
- THE DECEPTION OF COUNTERFEIT APPROACHES TO CHANGE
- THE REWARDS OF PURSUING GENUINE FELLOWSHIP WITH GOD

WEEK FOUR	SECTION FOUR

- THE BIBLICAL FRAMEWORK FOR DIAGNOSING AND DEALING WITH MAN'S MENTAL UNSOUNDNESS
- *READ THE HEART OF MAN AND THE MENTAL DISORDERS (EFFECTS OF SIN AND RIGHTEOUSNESS, BASIC RIGHTEOUSNESS AND BASIC SIN, MOVING FROM UNLOVING TO LOVING CH2-CH5)*

WEEK FIVE	SECTION FIVE
	- THE BIBLICAL FRAMEWORK FOR DIAGNOSING AND DEALING WITH MAN'S MENTAL UNSOUNDNESS
- THE PLACE OF LOVE IN DIAGNOSING AND DEALING WITH MAN'S MENTAL SOUNDNESS
- UNDERSTANDING ANGER
- *READ THE HEART OF MAN AND THE MENTAL DISORDERS (THE FOUR KINDS OF LOVE, AGAPE LOVE AND ITS ABSENCE, IMMATERIAL EFFECTS OF LOVING, IMMATERIAL EFFECTS OF NOT LOVING CH16-CH 17, CH 19-CH 24, ANGER CH 15)*
WEEK SIX	SECTION SIX
	- EXPRESSION OF LOVE
- THE FOUR KINDS OF HUMAN RELATIONSHIPS
- CHARACTERISTICS OF GOD TO EMBRACE
- 7 HABITS OF EFFECTIVE CHRISTIANS
- HOW TO BE A MATURE CHRISTIAN
- LIVING FOR THE GLORY OF GOD, REVIEW OF BIBLICAL COUNSELING FRAMEWORK
- *READ THE HEART OF MAN AND THE MENTAL DISORDERS (OPEN LOVE CH25-CH29)*
WEEK SEVEN	SECTION SEVEN
	- THE CONSCIENCE AND BIBLICAL COUNSELING
- TRUE GUILT VS. FALSE GUILT
- *READ THE HEART OF MAN AND THE MENTAL DISORDERS (CONSCIENCE CH6-CH11)*
WEEK EIGHT	SECTION EIGHT
	- EMOTIONS
- CATEGORIES OF JOY AND SORROW
- *READ THE HEART OF MAN AND THE MENTAL DISORDERS (EMOTIONS, JOY AND SORROW CH12-14)*

WEEK NINE	SECTION NINE

- THE TYPES OF FEARS MENTIONED IN THE BIBLE
- FEAR OF WORRY VS. FEAR OF GOD'S JUDGMENT (ANXIETY)
- EXPRESSIONS OF LACK OF LOVE, SENSE OF GUILT, AU FEAR, AU FLEEING
- BIBLICAL DIAGNOSIS OF MENTAL DISORDERS USING THE BIBLICAL FRAMEWORK
- AREAS IN OUR LIVES WHERE WE CAN FIND THE LACK OF LOVE
- BIBLICAL DIAGNOSIS USING THE BIBLICAL FRAMEWORK
- *READ THE HEART OF MAN AND THE MENTAL DISORDERS (HOW TO COUNSEL PP. 943-983 OLD EDITION PP. 1177-1223 NEW EDITION)*

WEEK TEN	SECTION TEN

- BIBLICAL VIEW OF SELF-ESTEEM, SELF IMAGE, SELF LOVE

WEEK ELEVEN	SECTION ELEVEN

- HOW THINKING CAN AFFECT THE BODY
- TWO LEVEL SINS
- HYPER-CRITICISM AND PERSONALITY CONFLICTS
- BIBLICAL DIAGNOSIS OF A PROBLEM USING THE BIBLICAL FRAMEWORK
- *READ THE HEART OF MAN AND THE MENTAL DISORDERS (SOMATO FORM DISORDERS PP. 571-582 OLD EDITION PP. 789-798 NEW EDITION, CH 35 TWO LEVEL SINS, PROJECTION, PROJECTIVE IDENTIFICATION PP. 545 OLD EDITION PP.759 NEW EDITION)*

WEEK TWELVE	SECTION TWELVE

- FORGIVENESS

WEEK THIRTEEN	SECTION THIRTEEN

- DECISION MAKING IN THE WILL OF GOD

WEEK FOURTEEN	SECTION FOURTEEN

- DISTIGUISHING BETWEEN GOSSIP AND SHARING
- WHAT DO YOU DO WHEN AL TALKS TO BETTY ABOUT CARL?

Section One
Introduction

You Will Become Like Your Teacher
(Understanding Your World View)
(Luke 6:39-40)

I. Those That Follow Blind Guides Will Fall into Destruction (v39).
  A. Blind guides lead others by the tradition of man instead of the truth of God leading to destruction.
  B. Blind guides lead others by the trends of the world instead of the truth of Christ leading to destruction.
  C. Blind guides lead others by personal preferences instead of biblical precepts leading to destruction.

II. You Will Become like Those Who Teach You (v40).
  A. Whoever is teaching you is shaping your Perspective of life.
  B. Whoever is teaching you is shaping your Values in life.
  C. Whoever is teaching you is shaping your Direction in life.

III. You Are Either Being Taught by Satan or the Son of God (v40).
  A. Your conduct exposes if Satan or the Son of God is teaching you (v43).
  B. Your character exposes if Satan or the Son of God is teaching you (v44).
  C. Your conversation exposes if Satan or the Son of God is teaching you (v45).

IV. Therefore You Must Evaluate Your World View to Determine Who Is Your Teacher
  (World View—your understanding of God, the world, mankind and how they relate to each other)
  A. Where do you believe man/ the world comes from?
  B. What do you believe has gone wrong with the world?
  C. What do you believe we can do about it?
  D. What is the Definition of Truth?
  E. Who is God and how does He operate?
  F. What happens when you die?

V. **There Are Ten Key Areas Where You Can Determine if You Are Guided by Satan or the Son of God:**
   A. In your ***Philosophy***—your attempt to discover and explain what is real and how one knows; your attempt to understand and explain the way the world is designed to function; your attempt to explain the things we already know by experience but cannot give clarity to feelings, thoughts, sense of right and wrong, etc.
   B. In your ***Theology***—your understanding of the existence, nature, and character of God
   C. In your view of ***Biology***—your understanding of nature and life
   D. In your view of ***Psychology***—your understanding of the soul
   E. In your ***Ethics***—your understanding what is right and wrong universally
   F. In your view of ***Sociology***—your understanding of social institutions and society; how you think we should live together and how you think society should be structured
   G. In your view of the ***Law***—what you believe the principles of conduct or procedure are expected to be observed by mankind in his society
   H. In your ***Politics***—how you believe the city, state, or nation should be governed
   I. In your view of ***Economics***—how you believe individuals or societies should govern their resources by an individual or by a society
   J. In your view of ***History***—your understanding of past places, persons and events

(For more study on Worldview get the series, *"Thinking Like a Christian"* from Summit Ministries)

VI. **The Deception of Satan**
   A. Satan through his doctrine of demons has led people to believe that man is basically good, society is bad and that bad behavior is a result of a bad society not a sinful nature in man.
   B. Satan through his doctrine of demons has lead people to believe that society needs to be reconstructed not that man needs to be redeemed and sanctified because he is basically good. Therefore the world is led to believe that people can and should be shaped and manipulated like objects to fit a society as needed.
   C. Satan through his doctrine of demons has lead people to believe that social problems are not moral problems but technical problems to be addressed by scientific solutions. Therefore the world believes that social planners and controllers are the key to remaking human nature and society not Redemption, Sanctification, and Restoration of mankind and society through Jesus Christ and His agenda for living.

D. Satan through his doctrine of demons has led people to reject the fact that the soul, the conscience, moral reasoning and moral responsibility are issues to be concerned with. He has lead people to believe that the direction of mankind and the culture rest in the hands of the social scientist and the government instead of Jesus Christ our God and Savior.

(Insights from the section adapted from <u>How Now Shall We live</u> by Charles Colson)

Key Point: *Your view of counseling will be determined by your worldview. The more biblical your worldview, the more biblical your counseling will be. The less biblical your worldview, the less biblical your counseling will be. Your teacher will determine your counseling since "no student is above his teacher but when fully trained will be like his teacher." You must determine if your view of counseling has been shaped by Satan or the Son of God!*

<u>Seven Key Questions We Can Use to Evaluate if a Counseling Model Is Guided by Satan or the Son of God?</u>

1. What are the philosophical assumptions about life and God that undergird this model of counseling? (Humanism, Naturalism, Theism, etc.)

2. What is the belief about of the nature of man (model of personality) in this model of counseling?

3. What is the belief about what is wrong with mankind (model of abnormality) in this model of counseling?

4. What is the belief about what makes a healthy /whole human being (model of health) in this model of counseling?

5. What is their method (model of counseling) of leading a person to their view of a healthy/ whole human being in this model of counseling?

6. What are their tangible measures (demonstrated effectiveness) to determine success in achieving their goal of a healthy/whole human being?

7. Where does this model contradict, compete with, or complement what the Bible says about life, God, the nature or man, a healthy whole human being? Where does this model contradict or compete with what the Bible says in their methodology and view of success?

Three Major Schools of Thoughts in Counseling

1. ***Psychological Counseling***—combines human observations with human wisdom to construct a system of counsel to help man deal with his problems and issues of life. This type of counseling is generally practiced by non-believers and Christians who accept psychological theories as an avenue to help people.

2. ***Integration Counseling***— combines human observation, human wisdom, and the Bible to construct a system of counsel to help man deal with his problems and issues of life. This is sometimes called "Christian Counseling." This type of counseling is generally practiced by Christians who believe that the Bible should be supplemented with psychological theories in order to help people.

3. ***Biblical Counseling***— takes the Bible to construct a system of counsel to help man deal with his problems and issue of life. This type of counseling is generally practiced by Christians who believe that the Bible has all we need to provide solutions to life's non organic, immaterial and what the world calls psychological problems and to help man function as God intended in all aspects of life.

(Insights from the section adapted from Biblical Counseling CD series by Rich Thomson)

So Why Promote Biblical Counseling above the others?

Key Point: *The Bible gives us all we need for mental soundness and for understanding and dealing with the basic needs of the inner, immaterial man. God's word instructs us to find from Scripture alone our principles for living, our understanding of human attitudes, motives, behaviors, and our solutions for man's, non organic, immaterial, inner problems and what the world calls psychological problems.*

1. We are warned in Scripture not to trust human wisdom for principles for living, understanding of human attitudes, motives, behaviors, and our solution for man's inner problems (problems that are non organic in nature). See Psalm 1:1-2 and Colossians 2:8.

2. We are warned in Scripture not to trust our own wisdom because we can be deceived by our own wisdom. See Proverbs 3:5-6; 14:12; 16:2, 25; 21:2, and Jeremiah 17:9.

3. We are instructed in Scripture that God's wisdom is superior to man's wisdom. Therefore, man's wisdom should not be added to God's wisdom as solutions to man's inner problems (Problems that are non organic in nature). See 1Corinthians 1:21, 25; 2:2-5, 3:20, and Isaiah 55:8-11.

4. We are instructed in Scripture that God's wisdom is sufficient to counsel the inner Person (the immaterial aspect of man). See Psalm 119:24, 99, 100, Hebrews 4:12, and Psalm 19:7-11.

(Insights from the section adapted from *The Heart of Man and the Mental Disorders* by Rich Thomson)

Why is it Futile to Mix Human Wisdom with the Bible?

Key Point: *The Idea of integrating human wisdom and the Bible in counseling the inner man is contradictory to Scripture. The reasons given for integrating human wisdom and the Bible are contradictory to Scripture.*

I. **Reason A:** We should integrate because Scripture shows that man should gain insight on his inner self by observation.

Response: On the contrary, God's Word warns man not to trust in his own insight about himself concerning his inner man. When Scripture acknowledges man's observation about himself as true, it is saying simply that man's observation must be included in the Bible in order for man to know that the observations are true. See Psalm 1:1-2, Colossians 2:8, Proverbs 3:5-6; 14:12; 16:25; 24:30-34, Jeremiah 17:9, Isaiah 55:8-11, 1Corinthians 15:33 (written by a playwright confirmed as true by Scripture; his name was Menander) Acts 17:28 (written by a poet but confirmed as true by Scripture) Titus 1:12-13 (referenced a pagan prophet but confirmed as true by Scripture)

II. **Reason B:** We should integrate because "all truth is God's truth."

Response: Scripture says, however, that man can easily deceive himself and should not trust his own assessments. He needs truth revealed from the One Who knows all truth in order to be sure man's "truth" is actually truth. See John 14:26; 16:13; 17:17, Proverbs 3:5-6, 2 Corinthians 12:12, Hebrews 2:3-4, and Mark 16: 17-20.

III. **Reason C:** We should integrate because human observations are general revelation from God, which supplement His special revelation in the Bible.

Response: This is a misrepresentation of general revelation. God's Word describes general revelation as revelation about God (not specifically about man), which is given to mankind in general through nature, providence, and conscience. As such, all of God's general revelation to mankind is also revealed through His special revelation in the Bible plus much, much more. See Psalm 19:1-6, Romans 1:18-20; 2:14-15, and Acts 14:17. Also see <u>Basic Theology</u>, Ryrie, pp. 28, 33 <u>The Moody Handbook of Theology</u>, 1993, pp.186-87.

IV. Reason D: We should integrate because just as it is acceptable to rely upon an unbelieving plumber or surgeon or auto mechanic, it is acceptable to receive counsel from human wisdom concerning the problems in our lives.

Response: Plumbing, surgery and autos are physical things not spiritual things. God's Word tells believers not to rely upon the wisdom of man to meet the inner problems of their lives. Christians are not promised perfect physical health or perfect plumbing but they are promised perfect peace. See Psalm 1:1-2, Colossians 2:8, Proverbs 3:5-6, and Isaiah 26:3.

V. Reason E: We should integrate because we are to "spoil the Egyptians" as Israel did by taking the best of human wisdom and leaving the rest.

Response: Scripture says however that Israel took the physical gold, silver, and jewels, not the philosophy of life from the Egyptians. God was seeking to change their philosophy. Believers are not to take the philosophy of life that comes from world. See Psalm 1:1-2 and Colossians 2:8.

VI. Reason F: We should integrate because there are some people who can only grow spiritually if human wisdom removes the barriers to growth within them.

Response: If this is true it implies that Scripture is insufficient to help one grow. It also implies that we need human wisdom and the Scripture in order to help one grow. God's Word says, however, that spiritual growth depends entirely upon a person's relationship with God and His Word not upon human wisdom. Human wisdom denies sin as the problem and places responsibility on outside uncontrollable responses. See 2 Timothy 3:16-17, 2 Peter 3:18, James 1:2-4, Ephesians 4:15, 1 Timothy 1:5, 1 Peter 2:2, and 2 Peter 1:5-8.

(Insights from the section adapted from *The Heart of Man and the Mental Disorders* by Rich Thomson)

So Why Promote Biblical Counseling Above the Other Counseling in the Church?

I. God has given us the answers to the most fundamental questions pertaining to man through His Word (See 2Peter 1:1-3, 2Timothy 3:16-17, Jeremiah 17:9-10, and Hebrews 4:12-13).

The Word of God answers questions such as:
- What is the nature of man and what is his relationship to God?
- What is man's fundamental problem?
- How should we and how do we relate to our fellow human beings?
- What values should guide and what values do guide our attitudes and actions?
- How can man solve his basic problems?
- What specific changes should he make?
- Who/what is the agent for such change?
- What are the goals of these changes?

II. Biblical counseling focuses on helping people deal with the heart issues that drive the behavioral issues as explained by God in His Word (See James 3:13-4:10, Luke 6:43-45, Matthew 6:19-21, and Ezekiel 14:1-11).

III. Biblical counseling focuses on helping people turn from sin in their thoughts, words, actions and relationships as prescribed by God in His Word. (See Colossians 3:5-9, Ephesians 4:17-22, 1John 1:9, Proverbs 28:13-14).

IV. Biblical counseling focuses on helping people walk in Christ's Righteousness in their thoughts, words, actions, and relationships as prescribed by God in His Word (See Galatians 5:16-25, Ephesians 4:23-32, Colossians 3:10-25, and Romans 12:1-3).

V. Biblical counseling's goal is to facilitate the process of one becoming like Christ in all aspects of life (See Ephesians 4:11-16 and Colossians 1:28-29).

VI. Biblical Counseling leads a person into truth that comes from God and not human observations and theories that are an antithesis to Scripture (See Matthew 28:18-20, 1Timothy 6:3-6, and 2Peter 1:16-21).

VII. Biblical Counseling is a way to lead unbelievers to Christ as you share with them their ultimate problem (sin) and their true need salvation (See Matthew 28:18-20).

VIII. Biblical Counseling is a way to help individuals in your Church grow spiritually as you share with them their problem (sin) and their solution—putting off sin and Putting on Righteousness (See 2Peter 1:1-10).

IX. Biblical Counseling is a way to provide the community with God's Solution's to life's problems (See Colossians 1:28-29).

X. True Biblical Counseling will demonstrate:
  A. A high View of God in His Character, Nature, Attributes etc.

  B. A high view in the Sufficiency of Scripture

  C. An accurate anthropology

  D. A Biblical understanding of the purpose of the Church

  E. A Biblical view of Church Leadership

  F. Insight that is based on Biblical foundations

  G. Methodologies that are based on Biblical foundations

  H. Goals that are God-centered instead of man centered

(Concept X adapted from Lance Quinn Senior Pastor of Little Rock Bible Church)

Section Two

Key Point: *If we assume that it is necessary to integrate human wisdom and the Bible, we give rise to logical conclusions which are contradicted by the Scripture.*

I. **Reason A**: If integration is necessary, the logical conclusion is that God has made us to depend upon human wisdom in addition to His wisdom for our inner lives.

   Response: God's Word says that we should depend upon His wisdom alone. The basic systems of psychology are developed by unbelievers. Therefore we should not listen to it or be held captive by it (See Psalm 1:1-3, Colossians 2:8, Proverbs 3:5-6; 14:12; 16:25).

II. **Reason B:** If integration is necessary, then the logical conclusion is that the Apostles and Prophets were somehow handicapped in their inner persons since we have much greater knowledge than they concerning the inner self.

   Response: The Scripture presents the opposite picture, however. The Apostles and Prophets had all they needed for their inner persons (See Philippians 4:11-13, Hebrews 11:32-37, 1 Corinthians 2:1-5, 2 Corinthians 12:9-10, Acts 7:54-60, and 2 Timothy 3:16-17).

III. **Reason C:** If integration is necessary, then the logical conclusion is that the fruit of the Spirit is not enough as we meet the trials and challenges of life.

   Response: The Holy Spirit is enough but we don't walk enough in the Holy Spirit (See 1 Corinthians 10:13, Proverbs 18:4, 2 Timothy 3:16-17, 2 Corinthians 4:7-9, and Galatians 5:22-23)

(Insights from section adapted from <u>The Heart of Man and The Mental Disorders</u> by Rich Thomson)

Key Point: *God's Word reveals that man's inner mental soundness is directly connected to those things for which he is responsible to God in his immaterial being, not with those things for which he is not responsible. (Human wisdom blames the brain for that which the Bible holds the heart responsible.)*

I. As created in the image of God, man, until death, is an inseparable unity of the material (body and brain) and the immaterial (heart or soul and spirit).
   A. We have been designed with a mind which involves our thoughts, beliefs, understanding, memory, judgment, imaginations, discernment and conscience (See Proverbs 23:7, Romans 12:2-3, Romans 2:15-16, Mark 2:6, and 2Corinthians 10:5).
   B. We have been designed with affections which involves our longings, desires, and feelings (See Psalm 20:4, Ecclesiastes 7:9, 11:9, Psalm 73:7, James 3:14, Hebrews 12:3, and Joshua 14:8).
   C. We have been designed with a will which involves our ability to choose and determine action (See Deuteronomy 30:19, Joshua 24:15, Psalm 25:12, and Ecclesiastes 2:4-8).
   D. Our mind, affections, and will, are the sum total of what we call the immaterial part of man (non-physical); The bible generally uses the words soul, spirit, and heart when speaking of the immaterial aspect of man (See 1Corinthains 2:11, Roman 8:16, and Proverbs 4:23) (Sometimes the word soul is used to describe the whole person both material and immaterial (See Acts 2:41)
   E. We have been designed with a physical body which is the home of the immaterial part of us (See 2Corinthains5:1-10, Philippians1:19-23, 1Corinthains9:27, and 1Corinthians 15:35-58).
   F. The physical body and immaterial part of man are an inseparable union while man is alive on earth (See Genesis 2:7, 1Corinthians 15:35-38, Philippians 1:19-23).
   G. We have been created as an eternal being that will live forever either in fellowship with God or in eternal damnation (See Luke 16:19-31, John 3:36, and Revelation 20:11-15).
   H. We are accountable to God for our thoughts, words, and deeds (See 2 Corinthians 5:10, Romans 14:10-12, and Ecclesiastes 12:13-14).
   I. There is a distinction between the heart (soul and spirit) and the body; the heart (soul and spirit) is the real you and the body is the house in which the real you lives (See Genesis 1:26, 2 Corinthians 5:6-10, and Philippians 1:19-23).

II. Inside man's immaterial heart there is his individual personality which is not confined to his material body and brain. Our individual personality keeps on living even after we die (See Revelation 6:9-11, 1 Samuel 28:15-19, and Luke 16:23-31; 9:28-31).

III. Man's immaterial heart interfaces with his material brain in the area of thought. We need both the immaterial heart and material brain for the thought process to happen while we are living. Thought processes go on in the immaterial heart and the material brain while we are living. When we die thought processes continue in the immaterial heart.

    A. Daniel 2:28 (He was thinking thoughts in his material brain.)

    B. Daniel 2:30 (He was thinking thoughts in immaterial heart.)

    C. Song of Solomon 5:2 (Mind was awake while brain was unconscious.)

IV. Man's material body and brain may limit or expand his ability to think or experience things here on earth, but the body and brain do not determine those thoughts, words, or actions which man is responsible before God to choose in his immaterial heart. Some of us have great intellect, small intellect, and some are retarded but these issues do not affect the processes of the immaterial heart. Sin is not caused by the brain or brain chemicals but by the thought processes of the immaterial heart. Therefore, if there is an issue of sin in our lives we must blame the immaterial heart and not the material body and brain. Medicine may deal with the symptoms of the problem but not root issues (See Matthew 15:17-20, Mark 7:18-23, Proverbs 4:23, Philippians 4:8, Galatians 5:19-23, Proverbs 18:14, and 1 Corinthians 10:13).

(Insights from this section adapted from The Heart of Man and The Mental Disorders by Rich Thomson)

The Three Basic Responses to People and Circumstances

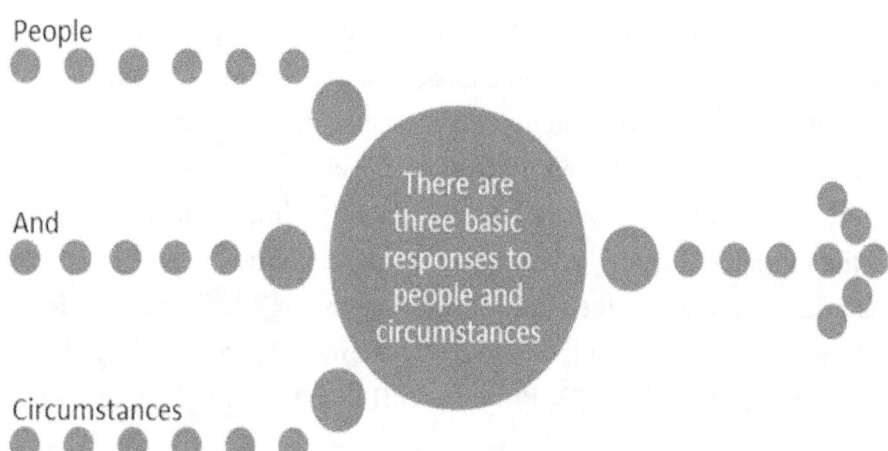

What I Can't and Can Control

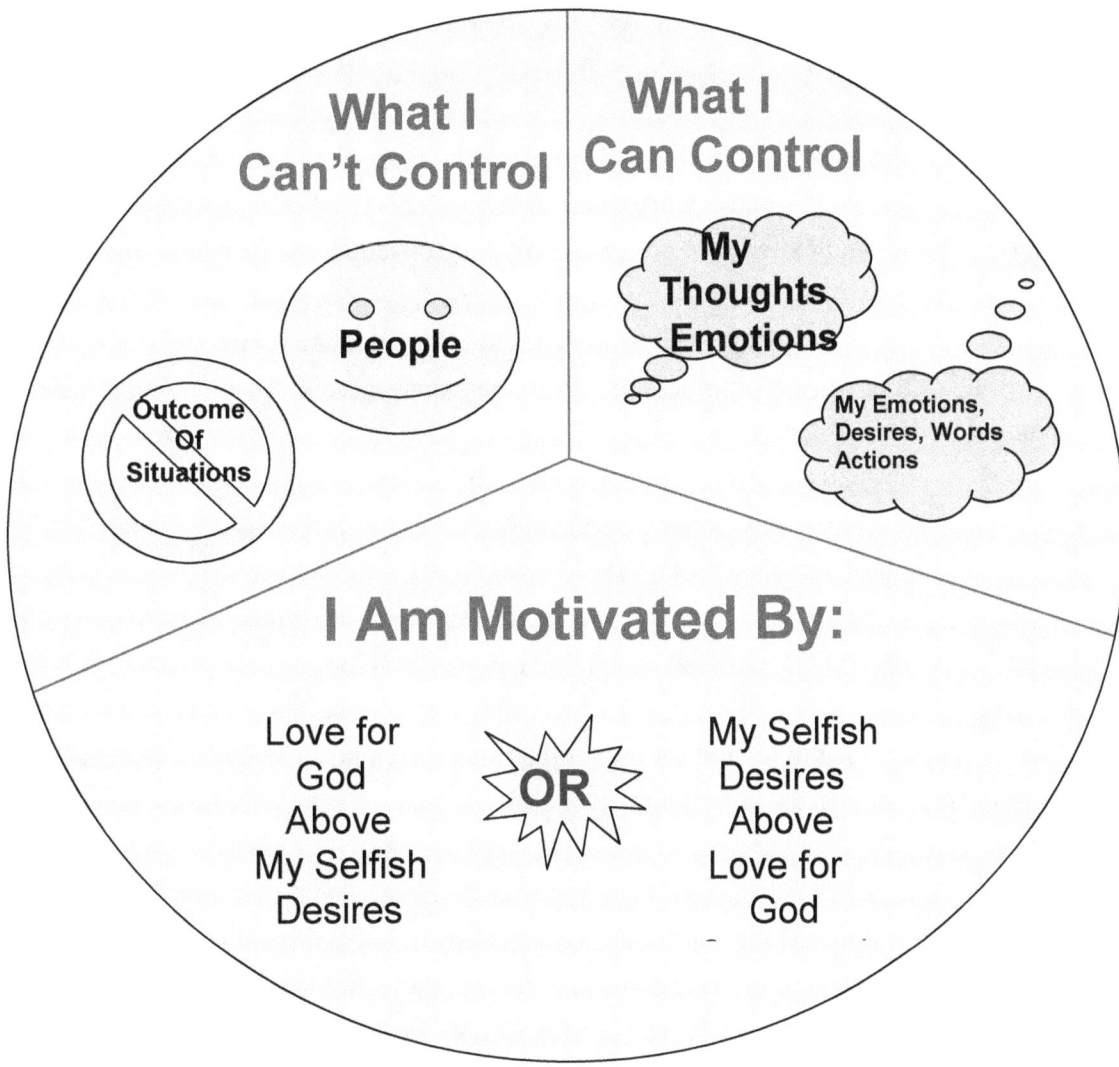

We cannot control people or the outcome of situations (Ecclesiastes 3:1-11, 7:13-14, 9:1-2.) We can only control our own thoughts, emotions, desires, words, and actions. (Romans 12:2-3, Proverbs 16:32, Psalm 37:4, Ephesians 4:29, 22-24) Therefore, we need to evaluate and take responsibility for how we are responding to people and the outcome of situations. (Galatians 6:7-8, 5:16-25) We need to evaluate what is motivating us with people and the outcome of situations. (James 1:13-14, 3:13-16, 4:1-3). Are we motivated by love for God above our selfish desires? Or, are we motivated by our selfish desires above love for God? (1John 2:15-16, James 4:4, James 3:16)

Key Point: *God's Word reveals that man is not responsible to God for some things which involve his material body and brain and his immaterial heart, but he is responsible for other things which involve them.*

I. Man is not necessarily responsible to God for what happens to him. See Acts 14:17, Matthew 5:45, Job 1:13-19; 2:7, and 2 Corinthians 6:4-5; 11:23-29. (The exception is when there is a reaping and sowing experience brought on by the consequences of your choices)

II. Man is not necessarily responsible to God for the pleasure or pain he experiences in his material body or for the happiness or sorrow he experiences in his immaterial heart and in his material body and brain.
    a.   Job 1:20 (Job was not responsible for his sorrow.)
    b.   Job 2:13 (Job was not responsible for the grief or pain.)
    c.   Ephesians 4:30 (no sin in grieving)
    d.   Matthew 26:37 (not responsible for grief or distress)
    e.   Proverbs 13:12, Romans 12:15, 1 Peter 2:21-23

III. Man is not responsible to God for the temptations which he experiences. (Exception is if a person sets himself up to be tempted.) See Matthew 4:1-11, Genesis 3:1-6, and Job 1:20; 2:3-6.

IV. Man is responsible to God for those thoughts, words, and actions for which he is said to be personally responsible in Scripture and for their results in his immaterial heart and in his material body. See Genesis 3:6-10, Psalm 32:3-4; 38: 1-10, Proverbs 28:1, and Proverbs 19:3.

V. Job was responsible for worship, not sinning against God, not cursing God, correcting the situation, yielding to God, repenting, evil thoughts, being critical, anger, complaining, arguing with God, blaming God, rebellion, rebuking God and trying to correct God. See Job 1:20-22; 2:9-10; 42:1-6; Job 3:3; 20, 23; 10:1-2, 13:3; 19:6; 23:2; 40:2.

(Insights from this section adapted from <u>The Heart of Man and The Mental Disorders</u> by Rich Thomson)

Key Point: *Man and animals are entirely different in this regard. Animals are not created in the image of God and are not personally responsible to God to choose their thoughts and actions, but they are determined by their instincts, environment, genetics, bodily urges, brain chemicals, present body condition, training, and past experiences. Man, on the other hand, is responsible to God not to allow the above things to determine the choices he makes regarding the thoughts, words, and actions for which he is personally responsible to God. That is, man's predispositions are not to determine the reactions of his immaterial heart. (We are predisposed but not predetermined.)*

The Personality of Man

Read and analyze these scriptures: Revelation 6:9-11, Luke 9:28-31, 1Samuel 28:15-19 and make a list of things which are usually associated with man's brain but which in these instances are exhibited by people who are physically dead and have only their immaterial beings to account for them:

Characteristics normally tied to the brain of the living:
    A.
    B.
    C.
    D.
    E.
    F.
    G.
    H.
    I.
    J.
    K.
    L.
    M.
    N.
    O.

First Key Point: After doing the observation we find that many of those characteristics we assume are limited to the brain are not. Man's immaterial heart interfaces with his material brain while he functions on earth. After death many functions we associate with the brain continue in operation in man's immaterial being. The heart chooses and the brain is involved but it is the heart that drives the choices not the brain. Man's immaterial heart is the control center of those things for which man is responsible to God. Inside man's immaterial heart there is his individual personality which is not confined to his material body and brain. Our individual personality keeps on living even after we die.(Revelation 6:9-11, 1 Samuel 28:15-19, Luke 9:28-31)

Second Key Point: Man's material body and brain may limit or expand his ability to think or experience things here on earth, but the body and brain do not determine those thoughts, words, or actions which man is responsible before God to choose in his immaterial heart. Some of us have great intellect, small intellect, and some are retarded but these issues do not affect the processes of the immaterial heart. Sin is not caused by the brain or brain chemicals but by the thought processes of the immaterial heart. Therefore, if there is an issue of sin in our lives we must blame the immaterial heart and not the material body and brain. Medicine may deal with the symptoms of the problem but not root issues (See Matthew 15:17-20, Mark 7:18-23, Proverbs 4:23).

(Insight adapted from <u>The Heart of Man and The Mental Disorders</u> by Rich Thomson)

Responsible or Not

Place these items in the categories below that best fit:

Disappointment, worry, loss of loved one, sense of guilt, forgiving/ unforgiving attitudes, interest in opposite sex, peace of God, not being loving, sense of being hurt, sexual imaginations/lust, being afraid of God's punishment, genetic weakness, negativism/hope, not being loved, psychosomatic bodily problems, grumbling, physical pain/pleasure, thankfulness/thanklessness, embarrassment

A. Things for which man is not responsible to God as being right or wrong (neutral):

B. Things for which man is responsible to God (right or wrong in the sight of God):

C. Results in one's life from the right or wrong thoughts, attitudes, words, or actions

(Idea adapted from Rich Thomson)

Section Three

Key Point: *God's Word promises that the mental soundness which people seek in counseling is a result of a present, intimate relationship with God in Jesus Christ. Peace is a result living a Christ-Centered Life. A Christ- Centered Life can be defined as a life that is devoted to trusting God, confession and repentance of sin in order to know Jesus Christ intimately, to become like Jesus Christ in character, conduct, and conversation, and to be useful to Christ in all aspects of life. This all done through the Power of the Holy Spirit who produces the peace which people seek in counseling. The author of Peace is God yet we look to the world (which denies God) to provide it. Generally the idea is "Would you help me change others so I can have peace?" If there is a lack of peace in someone's life, there is a lack in their relationship with God. In order to find out where the lack is we would listen to them and see what has happened to them. We would also listen, to identify: (1) things they are not responsible for, (2) how they are reacting to circumstances, and (3) things for which they are responsible before God. As we identify the areas of thought, words, and deeds where they are reacting in sin, we will find what is robbing them of their peace. If they act appropriately in these areas towards God (as He has commanded) they will find the peace. Again peace comes from my relationship with God not my relationship with others. Therefore, I must have a genuine relationship with God through His saving Grace in order to experience this kind of peace. Saving Grace does not produce a license to live any way we want and bank on the salvation from Christ as security that we are still going to heaven; Saving Grace teaches us to deny ourselves the worldliness that corrupts us so that we may pursue the Godliness that changes us into the image of Jesus Christ thereby enjoying the peace of God that comes through genuine fellowship with Him. If you are claiming salvation but living like people who do not belong to Christ either you are suffering from Spiritual Amnesia, or Spiritual Deception which results in a lack peace. Meaning, either you have forgotten that you have been saved to know Christ, to become like Christ and to be useful to Christ, or you are really not a Christian but have been deceived into thinking you are. Experiencing the saving grace of God should lead us to consistency in denying self and a stable God-ordered life resulting in experiencing the peace of God. In order to experience the peace of God on a consistent basis, we must understand the centrality of salvation, avoid spiritual amnesia, avoid counterfeit change and purse genuine fellowship with the Christ.*

The Centrality of Salvation
(Titus 2:11-14)

I. God's grace has appeared v11

  A. In this text, God's grace is His beneficiary activity on behalf of humans.

  B. In this text, God's grace is Jesus Christ.

  C. In this text, God's grace is the death, burial, resurrection of Jesus Christ for the penalty of sin, power and sin and presence of sin that enslaves mankind; so that mankind may be delivered from sin, devoted to Christ, developed in Christ, and delighted in the return of Christ.

  D. God's beneficiary activity on behalf of humans has been brought to light/ made known through the Person and Work of Jesus Christ.

II. God's grace brings salvation to all types of people v11

  A. Salvation is deliverance from the penalty of sin – deliverance from the separation from God forever in eternal damnation to burn forever in the lake of fire.

  B. Salvation is being delivered from the power of sin- deliverance from the slavery to evil; of being controlled by the evil desires of your heart.

  C. Salvation is being delivered from the presence of sin – to be set apart from evil and to dwell in the new heaven and new earth with Christ forever.

  D. God's grace which was revealed in the person and work of Jesus Christ has brought a deliverance from the penalty of sin, the power of sin, and one day the presence of sin to all who will receive it.

III. This grace of salvation not only delivers us from the penalty, power and one day presence of sin, but it teaches us to live in a such a manner that displays that we have been delivered from the penalty, power and one day presence of sin v12-v13

  A. Those who have received this grace of salvation are instructed to deny ungodliness – to turn away from living without respect, regard, resolve or reverence for the Character, Commands, and Commission of God.

B. Those who have received this grace of salvation are instructed to deny worldly desires – to turn away from unrestrained desires for things forbidden; turn away from wanting good things in this world in the wrong way (i.e. lusting, coveting) ; to turn away from the lust of flesh, the lust of the eyes and the pride of life.

C. Those who have received this grace of salvation are instructed to live sensibly – to live by good judgment based upon the standards of God, to stay within the limits and boundaries set by God in Scripture in relation to their character, conduct, conversation as well as commitments.

D. Those who have received this grace of salvation are instructed to live righteously- to live in such a way before people and with people that is deemed acceptable and pleasing to God according to Scripture.

E. Those who have received this grace of salvation are instructed to live godly – to live with devotion to and respect for Jesus Christ our God and Savior.

F. Those who have received this grace of salvation are to be genuinely anticipating the blessed hope and appearing of great God and Savior Jesus Christ – having a happy expectation of seeing Jesus Christ in the fullness of Character .

IV. Our God and Savior Jesus Christ (who is the means by which God the Father provided this grace of salvation) purchased us so that we may be severed from a life of sin, sanctified as His possession, serving with eagerness as He designed us to do so v14

A. We have been redeemed from every lawless deed – Jesus paid for every sin we have committed and could commit with His life; He purchased us for Himself by His crucifixion on the Cross, death, burial, and resurrection from His death on the Cross.

B. We are being purified to be a people of Christ possession – We have been set apart as Saints by calling and we are being set apart from sin to devotion to Him in lifestyle.

C. He is purifying us to be zealous for good deeds – we are being sanctified to serve as ambassadors for unbelievers and builders of Christ-like character in believers.

D. Salvation is not an end but a means to knowing, becoming like, and being useful to our Great and God and Savior Jesus Christ.

The Danger of Spiritual Amnesia
(2 Peter 1:1-9)

I. A Christian who lacks the spiritual qualities of moral excellence, knowledge, self control, perseverance, godliness, brotherly kindness, and love is blind or shortsighted v9

    A. A Christian who is blind or shortsighted is seeing only what is near.

    B. A Christian who is blind or shortsighted is lacking in a godly perspective of life; He does not interpret life situations through God's truth.

    C. A Christian who is blind or shortsighted has his mind set on things of this world with no serious thought to a godly interpretation of the things of this world.

II. A Christian who is blind or shortsighted has forgotten his purification from his former sins v9

    A. A Christian who has forgotten his purification from his former sins, is a Saint who has been living as if his past forgiveness of sin through Jesus Christ has no relevance to his present lifestyle.

    B. A Christian who has forgotten his purification from his former sins, is a Saint who is not living in practice what he is by position.

    C. A Christian who has forgotten his purification from his former sins, is a saint who has allowed the light of the world to dim his eyes to his conversion, connection, commitment and calling to Jesus Christ our Lord, God and Savior.

III. A blind, shortsighted Christian who has forgotten his purification from his former sins lacks a godly perspective on his: v9

    A. *Personhood in Christ-* Since this Christian has not embraced his identity in Christ, he tends to tie his identity to other people, his own performance, positions of authority, or he wants or has; This person has connected his identity to the temporal things of this world instead of the Character of Jesus Christ. He does not see himself as Christ sees him. This Christian does not evaluate himself, his roles, and his responsibilities according to God's perspective (1Samuel 15:1-24, Galatians 2:20).

B. *Provision in Christ* - This Christian is blind to the implications of his union with Christ. As a result he is dominated by indwelling sin, the world and the devil leading to instability in his life. He does not embrace the fact that he has been joined with Christ. Nor does this Christian embrace that in his relationship with Christ he has all he needs to live a proper, peaceful, productive life; He does not understand that this kind of life would result in grace and peace being multiplied to him through Christ, experiential knowledge of Christ, genuine Christ like character, and stability in his life. (James 1:5-8, 2Peter 1:1-8).

C. *Progressive sanctification in Christ* – This Christian may focus on past forgiveness of sin and future blessings in heaven, but he does not focus on the present pursuit of knowing Christ, becoming like Christ, and being useful to Christ. He lacks discernment of good and evil because he is lazy in his pursuit of truth and application thereof. This Christian does not understand that through his relationship and union with Christ he has been given the command and the power to turn from sin in thoughts, words and deeds and to walk in what is right in thoughts, words, and deeds so that he may know Christ intimately, become like Christ practically, and to be useful to Christ consistently (Hebrews 5:11-14, Ephesians 4:11-32).

IV. **A Christian who lacks a spiritual perspective on his personhood in Christ, his provision in Christ, and progressive sanctification in Christ may seek to fill in the gaps with God-replacements such as: (Jeremiah 2:13)**

   A. Formalism-Consistent participation in church meetings, ministries, and missions activities yet void of a transformed life from participating in these meetings, ministries, and missions activities because there is no genuine fellowship with Christ in these activities

   B. Legalism- Living a life of rules and regulations thinking one is right with God by keeping them yet void of a transformed life through them because there is no genuine fellowship with Christ; Trying to earn by works what can only be gained through grace and genuine fellowship with Jesus Christ

   C. Mysticism- Constantly hunting for a spiritual high, a dynamic encounter with God; reducing Christianity to the pursuit of dynamic emotional and spiritual experiences instead a pursuit of Jesus Christ yet void of a transformed life through these experience because there is no genuine fellowship with Christ in these experiences

   D. Biblicism-Pursuit of a high knowledge of the Bible; becoming a theological expert yet void of a transformed life because there is no seeking to know Christ, to become like Christ, and to be useful to Christ through the pursuit of a high knowledge of the Bible (James 1:22-24)

E. Socialism-Connecting with others in the Church for genuine fellowship, acceptance, respect and position yet void of a transformed life in these connections because they were reduced to an avenue for self fulfillment instead of being elevated to an avenue for mutual sanctification in Jesus Christ.

(Examples from the book <u>How People Change</u> by Timothy Lane and Paul Tripp)

The Deception of Counterfeit Approaches to Change
(Colossians 2:6, 8)

I. **We are called to walk with God in the manner in which we received Him (v6)**
   A. We received Jesus Christ by faith.

   B. We received Jesus Christ as Lord.

   C. Therefore we should continue to walk by faith in Christ since we receive Him by faith.

   D. Therefore we should continue to walk with Christ as Lord of our lives since we received Him as Lord of our lives.

II. **We are not to allow ourselves to be held captive by empty and deceptive philosophy (v8)**
   A. We are not to allow ourselves to be controlled by wisdom that is devoid of truth and futile.

   B. We are not to allow ourselves to be controlled by wisdom that is fruitless and without effect.

   C. We are not to allow ourselves to be controlled by wisdom that is based on the ideas of man.

   D. We are not to allow ourselves to be controlled by wisdom that is based on the world's basic principles.

III. **If we allow ourselves to be held captive by empty and deceptive philosophy we will find ourselves misguided in our relationship with Jesus Christ leading to pursuing counterfeit approaches to change in our lives. (Proverbs 14:12)**

> A. When held captive by empty and deceptive philosophy we will seek to change ourselves by trying to change others. "If my husband treated me better then I could be nicer." "If my children respected me then I could be a better parent." "If my Church would show more care and concern then I could be more committed." The deception in this philosophy is the belief that my sin and my change of sin is conditioned upon the lives of others. Truth is, sin choices come from the sinful motivations of our own hearts. True change is conditioned upon a changed position from sinner to saint and a changed heart through a genuine relationship with Jesus Christ.
>
> B. When held captive by empty and deceptive philosophy we will seek to change ourselves by trying to change our circumstances. "If I had more money I would be a better person." "If I could change my looks my life would be better." "If I were married I would be a good person." "If I were divorced my attitude would be better." The deception in this philosophy is the belief that the condition of my heart and life will be changed by different circumstances. Truth is, the condition of our hearts and lives will be changed by a changed position from sinner to saint and a changed heart through a genuine relationship with Jesus Christ.
>
> C. When held captive by empty and deceptive philosophy we will seek to change ourselves by trying to change our behavior apart from dealing with our hearts. "I am going to work on studying the Bible more." "I am going to work harder at being nicer to people" "I am going to work hard at not being angry." "I am going to work harder on not letting people get to me." The deception in this philosophy is the belief that skill development and behavior modification is all you need to have a changed life. Truth is, skill development and behavior modification do not address the motivation behind the behavior which is connected to the condition of our hearts. Trying to change behavior without dealing with motivation behind the behavior will lead to relapse to the bad behavior. Behavioral change must be joined with a heart change if it is going to be genuine change. This can only happen by a changed position from sinner to saint and a changed heart through a genuine relationship with Jesus Christ.

D. When held captive by empty and deceptive philosophy we will seek to change ourselves by the pursuit of knowledge. "Knowledge is power." "The more I learn the better off I will be." "To know better is to do better." "If you would just read this book on the subject it will change your life." The deception in this philosophy is the belief that awareness of insight alone will change your life. Truth is, having knowledge without ability and interest to act on the knowledge will not change your life. You can know what is right and still live in sin because you do not value the truth or because you do not have the ability to apply it because you have not been set free from the power and penalty of sin. Unless you have been changed from sinner to saint and had a changed heart through a genuine relationship with Christ, you will not have interest or ability to act on the knowledge received as God designed. Our awareness must be connected with love for God and love for others in order to have a changed life. If not we will be puffed up by our knowledge instead of propped up through our knowledge.

The Rewards of Pursuing Genuine Fellowship with God

I. Through fellowship with God

A. We can experience peace for our minds (Isaiah 26:3, Galatians 5:22, John14:27, and Philippians 4:6-7).

B. We can gain strength and sufficiency in Christ to meet any kind of internal or external circumstances which comes into our lives (1 Corinthians 10:13, 2 Corinthians 4:7-9, and Philippians 4:11-13).

C. We can gain confidence in Him (Trusting God) and confidence before Him (Assurance that we are alright with God) in whatever situation we find ourselves (Psalm 27: 1-3; 46:1-3, Hebrews 13:5-6, Proverbs 14:26; 28:1, and 1 John 3:21, 4:17-18).

D. We have the ability through His love to love unconditionally in whatever situation we find ourselves (Romans 5:8; 8:35-39, Galatians 5:22, 1John 3:15-23, and 1John 4:7-21).

E. We have the ability to walk in hope and optimism in any present or future situation (Romans 5:1-5; Hebrews 6:13-20, 13:5-6, and 1John 3:1-3).

F. We can obtain inner joy from God Himself—a joy which is not dependent upon our bodily feelings or our past, present, or future circumstances. This joy is not available to unbelievers. The context determines whether it is human happiness or God's joy (Galatians 5:22, 1 Thessalonians 1:6, and Acts 13:51-52).

G. We have the ability to relate rightly to God, to others and to the world with sensible attitudes, words, and actions. If I am called to be sensible it suggest that I am responsible for being insensible which suggests that sanity and insanity are in the realm of my responsibility (2Timohty 3:16, Ephesians 5:1-33, Titus 2:1-6, Romans 12:1-21, 1Peter 2: 1-25, Ephesians 6:1-9, and 1Peter 3:1-12).

H. We have the ability to come to know ourselves thoroughly (Matthew 16:24-26, John 8:31-32, Romans 2:14-15, Proverbs 20:5, and 1John 4:6).

I. We have the ability to relate rightly to God, to others and to the world with sensible attitudes, words, and actions. If I am called to be sensible it suggest that I am responsible for being insensible which suggests that sanity and insanity are in the realm of my responsibility (2Timohty 3:16, Ephesians 5:1-33, Titus 2:1-6, Romans 12:1-21, 1Peter 2: 1-25, Ephesians 6:1-9, and 1Peter 3:1-12).

Ways We Are to relate to Each Other

Look at these passages of Scripture and identify and write down in each section 3-4 descriptions given as to how we are relate to each other. You are just surveying the chapters and providing a brief description.

Romans, Chapters 12 – 14
1.
2.
3.

Ephesians, Chapters 4-6
1.
2.
3.

Colossians, Chapters 3-4
1.
2.
3.

Philippians, Chapters 2-4
1.
2.
3.

Hebrews, Chapters 12-13
1.
2.
3.

1Peter, Chapters 2-5

1.

2.

3.

1John Chapters 1-4

1.

2.

3.

Key Point: If we applied these guidelines to the relationships we have, how different would our relationships be? How many marriages would be saved, friendships maintained, or even relationship staying Holy? We don't need the world to tell us how to relate to each other. We need to submit to what has been already commanded to us through the Word of God.

(Idea adapted from Rich Thomson)

Section Four

Key Point: *God's Word exposes a framework by which man can understand how his lack of peace, non-biological problems, and quality of life are tied to how he governs his thoughts, words, and deeds toward God and others.*

I. **Adam and Eve made a sinful Choice (See Genesis 3:1-13).**

   A. Adam and Eve chose to doubt the command given them by God.

   B. Adam and Eve chose to distrust the command given them by God.

   C. Adam and Eve chose to devalue the command given them by God.

   D. Adam and Eve chose to disengage from the command given them by God.

   E. Adam and Eve chose to disobey the command given them by God.

   F. Adam and Eve chose to deny their sinful behavior to God.

   G. Adam and Eve chose to defend their sinful behavior to God.

II. **Adam and Eve's sinful choice produced negative consequences in their souls resulting in negative consequences in the souls of mankind afterwards (See Genesis 3:1-13).**

   A. Sin lead Adam and Eve to experience a sense of guilt in their soul - the knowledge or awareness in your thoughts that you are disobedient which may or may not result in painful feelings, sorrow, or a self reproach (See Genesis 3:6-7).

   B. The sense of guilt brought about a fear of God's judgment in their soul—the anticipation of some misfortune or doom; a sense of anxiety or fear within when there is no apparent danger externally at the moment (See Genesis 3:8-10).

C. The guilt and fear of God's judgment in their soul led Adam and Eve to flee within their soul and within their actions—to seek to escape or get away from the negative thoughts or emotions within our soul when there is no apparent danger externally at the moment (See Genesis 3:7, 10-13).

D. When we choose to follow the direction of Adam and Eve in thoughts, words, or actions we will experience a sense of guilt in our souls—the knowledge or awareness in your thoughts that you are disobedient which may or may not result in painful feelings, sorrow, or a self reproach (See Romans 2:14-15 and 1John 3:21-22).

E. When we choose to follow the direction of Adam and Eve thoughts, words, or actions we will experience the fear of God's judgment in our souls—the anticipation of some misfortune or doom; a sense of anxiety or fear within when there is no apparent danger externally at the moment (See Acts 24: 24-25 and 1Jn 4:17-18).

F. When we choose to follow the direction of Adam and Eve in thoughts, words, or actions we tend to try to flee the negative thoughts and emotions from within our souls which resulted from the sin choice—to seek to escape or get away from the negative thoughts or emotions within our soul when there is no apparent danger externally at the moment (See Leviticus 26:17, 36-37).

```
              leads to                leads to                         leads to
Sin ----------→ Sense of Guilt --------→ Fear of God's Judgment ---------→ Fleeing
Choice         in our souls            in our souls                      in our souls and
                                                                         outside our souls
```

G. Most of the time when the word guilt is mentioned in the bible it is referring to the fact of guilt (the state of being wrong). However the sense of guilt is implied throughout scripture without using the word guilt. The sense guilt can be described as the knowledge or awareness of being wrong which may or may not result in painful feelings, sorrow, or a self reproach. When we refer to guilt we will be talking about a sense of guilt (See 1 John 3:21, Psalm 38:4, Matthew 26:75, Ps 51:17).

Summary:

Adam and Eve disobeyed God. Adam and Eve became aware of their nakedness and covered themselves. Adam and Eve heard God and tried to hide themselves because they knew they had done wrong and were afraid of what God would do to them. (What do we call this awareness of wrong?) God questioned Adam and Eve and gave them a chance to repent. Adam and Eve tried to connect being naked with their reason for hiding. Adam and Eve tried to hide behind justifications and blame. God tied nakedness to disobedience. Sin lead Adam and Eve to a sense of guilt. The sense of guilt brought about a fear of judgment. The fear of God's judgment led Adam and Eve to flee through loin coverings, to flee in the garden, and to flee through justification and blame.

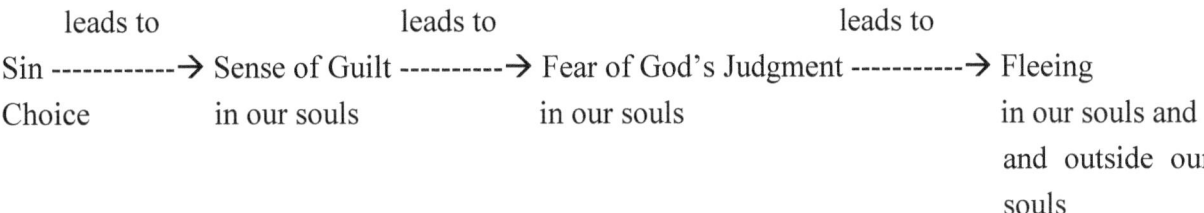

III. The Word of God exposes this concept even more through Proverbs 28:1.

A. In most two-line proverbs the first part of the verse implies something about the second part of the verse and the second part of the verse implies something about the first part of the verse.

B. The first part of Proverbs 28:1 talks about the wicked fleeing when no one is pursuing while the second part talks about the righteous being bold as a lion.

C. The wicked refers to persons who do not live their lives according to the standards of God.

D. The righteous refers to persons who do live their lives according to the standards of God.

E. The text is not referring to a positional righteousness or wickedness before God but the practice of righteousness and the practice of wickedness before God.

F. Those who are not lining up with God's Word try to escape or flee God's judgment. They seek to flee in thoughts, words, or actions from God's judgment.

G. They flee judgment when no one is pursuing them or when there is no apparent danger.

H. This implies that there is a sense of guilt and fear that is taking place inside the heart of the person which results in an effort to escape or flee in thoughts, words, or actions from God's judgment.

   Sin -------------→ Guilt ---------------→ Fear of Judgment --------------→ Fleeing

I. Those who are lining up with God's standard are confident or have a boldness that is associated with that of a lion.

J. This implies that there is the peace of God in the heart of the person which results in a confidence before God and a desire to draw near.

   1. This is a peace that results from confession, repentance, right choices, the fruit of the Spirit which is what we call the peace of God (See Isaiah 26:3; 57:15 and Philippians 4:5-10).

   2. This is not the peace that comes from justification—peace with God See (Romans 5:1-2).

   3. Unbelievers do not experience this kind of peace because it is the by product of the Holy Spirit who indwells believers and not unbelievers. However, they do experience a peace that derives from lining up with the work of law written on their hearts (See Galatians 5:16-26, Romans 2:14-15).

K. The righteous therefore tend to be bold or have confidence before God due to making choices that line up with the standards of God, which bring about the peace of God, for the believer, which brings about confidence before God for the believer, which results in drawing near to God instead of trying to flee from God for the believer.

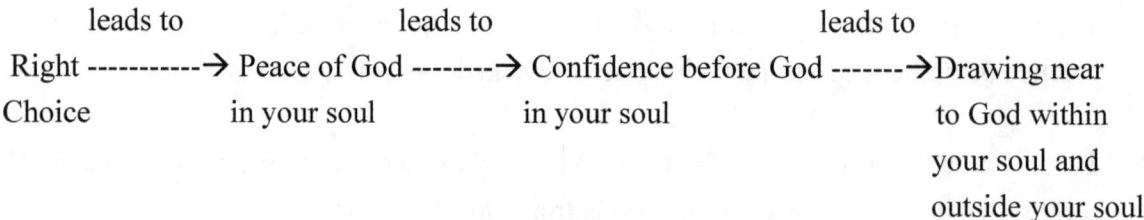

IV. How does the unbeliever handle a sense of guilt, apparently uncaused fear and apparently uncaused fleeing? Don't they have the peace of God, confidence before God, and a desire to draw near to God at times?

A. When a unbeliever has a sense of guilt, apparently uncaused fear or apparently uncaused fleeing and does not submit to Jesus Christ to save him from the penalty of sin, the power of sin and the presence of sin he will seek to :

1. Do good deeds to cover guilt thus receiving peace that comes from lining up with the work of the law written on his heart not the peace of God (See Romans 2:14-15).
2. Desensitize his conscience to the guilt of the sin through more sinful thoughts, words, and actions thus suppressing the truth in ungodliness and unrighteousness (See Ephesians 4:17-19 and Romans 1:18-32).
3. Pursue false religions seeking to find in those religions what can only be gained in Jesus Christ alone (See Romans 1:21-23).
4. Pursue the peace of the world thus receiving a peace that is contingent upon the world's system and temporal pleasures of this life instead of God (See John 14:27).
   a. Money
   b. Materials
   c. Medications
   d. Movies,
   e. Media
   f. Accomplishments
   g. Human Resources
   h. Entertainment

B. As an unbeliever does instinctively what is right according to the work of the law written on his heart it will aid in his mental soundness by delivering him from the negative effects of a sense of guilt, apparently uncaused fear, and apparently uncaused fleeing until the Holy Spirit convicts him of his sinful condition before a Holy God (See Romans 2:14-15. John 16:8-11).

C. The peace the unbeliever gets from doing what is right according to the work of the law written on his heart is not the peace of God but the peace of his conscience (See Romans 2:14-15).

D. The confidence the unbeliever has is based on self righteousness, and the result of lining up with the work on the law written on his heart not God's righteousness produced by faith in Jesus Christ (See Philippians 3:1-6 and Romans 2:14-15).

E. Unless the Holy Spirit convicts an unbeliever to draw near to accept Jesus Christ, he will be drawing near to a false god (See Romans 1:21-23).

F. If the unbeliever is not willing to submit to Christ he will seek to find peace through self-righteousness, the world's system/temporal pleasures, or false religion (See Philippians 3:1-6, 1John 2:15-17, John 14:27 and Romans 1:21-23).

V. **The Believer can move from walking in sin to walking in what is right before Jesus Christ our Lord through:**

A. Confessing sin (See 1 John 1:9).

B. Counting on God's forgiveness of the sin confessed (See 1 John 1:9 and Romans 8:1).

C. Allowing one's self to be controlled by the Holy Spirit through yielding one's self to God's power and precepts (See Ephesians 5:18, Galatians 5:16, and 2Peter 1:16-21).

D. Counting on the control of the Holy Spirit by walking by faith and not by sight. Which leads to walking in what is right and experiencing the by-product of walking in what is right by faith (See 2Corithians 5:1-9, and 1 John 5:1-13).

VI. **The Unbeliever can move from walking in sin to walking in what is right before Jesus Christ our Lord through:**

A. Confessing his/her sin and need to be forgiven of his/her sins through faith in the death burial and resurrection of Jesus Christ (See Acts 2:22-42 and Romans 10:5-13).

B. Counting on God's forgiveness of their sin unto salvation through faith in the death, burial resurrection of Jesus Christ (See Ephesians 1:7, John 3:16, and Romans 8:1).

C. Allowing one's self to be controlled by the Holy Spirit through yielding one's self to God's power and precepts (See Ephesians 5:18, Galatians 5:16, and 2Peter 1:16-21).

D. Counting on the control of the Holy Spirit by walking by faith and not by sight, which leads to walking in what is right and the results that follow (See 2Corithians 5:1-9 and 1 John 5:1-13).

VII. **God grants mercy and forgiveness when one confesses and repents of sin resulting in living as God commands thereby producing a quiet soul (See Proverbs 28:13).**

   A. To confess sin is to acknowledge or agree with God that you have sinned (See Psalm 32:3-5).

   B. To confess sin is to own up to your inappropriate thoughts, words, actions, or relational patterns as God has made you aware of them (See Psalm 51:1-4).

   C. To confess sin is to acknowledge to another that you were inappropriate in some word or action towards them (See James 5:16).

   D. To forsake or repent of sin is to have a change of mind towards the inappropriate thoughts, words, actions, or relational patterns, seeing the sin as God sees it (See 2Corinthians 7:9-11).

   E. To forsake or repent of sin is to turn away from practicing the inappropriate thoughts, words, actions, or relational patterns (See 2Corinthians 7:9-11).

   F. To forsake or repent of sin is to abandon the practice of the inappropriate thoughts, words, actions, or relational patterns (See 2Corinthians 7:9-11).

   G. When one confess and repents of his sin he will experience a sense of peace from God (See Isaiah 57:14-21 and 2Corinthains 7:10).

   H. As one chooses to live properly as a result of confessing and repenting of his sin he will experience a sense of confidence before God (See Psalm 32:5-11 and 1John 3:21-22).

I. As one chooses to live properly as a result of confession and repenting of his sin he will seek to draw near to God (See Psalm 63:1, Psalm 73:21-28).

```
         leads to              leads to                   leads to
Right ----------→ Peace of God --------→ Confidence before God -------→Drawing near
Choice            in your soul           in your soul                   to God within
                                                                        your soul and
                                                                        outside your soul
```

(Insights adapted from <u>The Heart of Man and The Mental Disorders</u> by Rich Thomson)

BIBLICAL COUNSELING FRAMEWORK

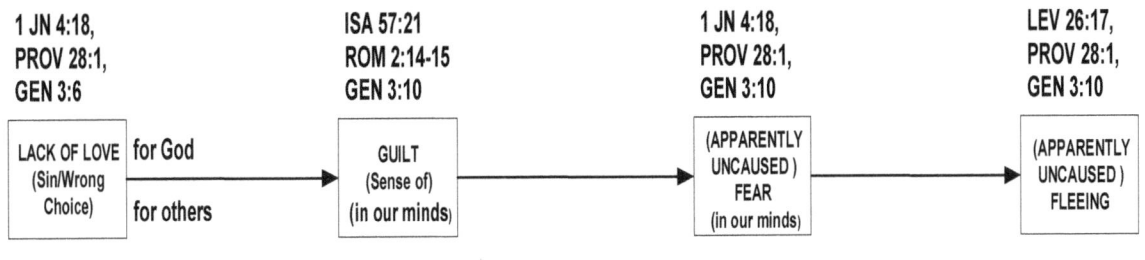

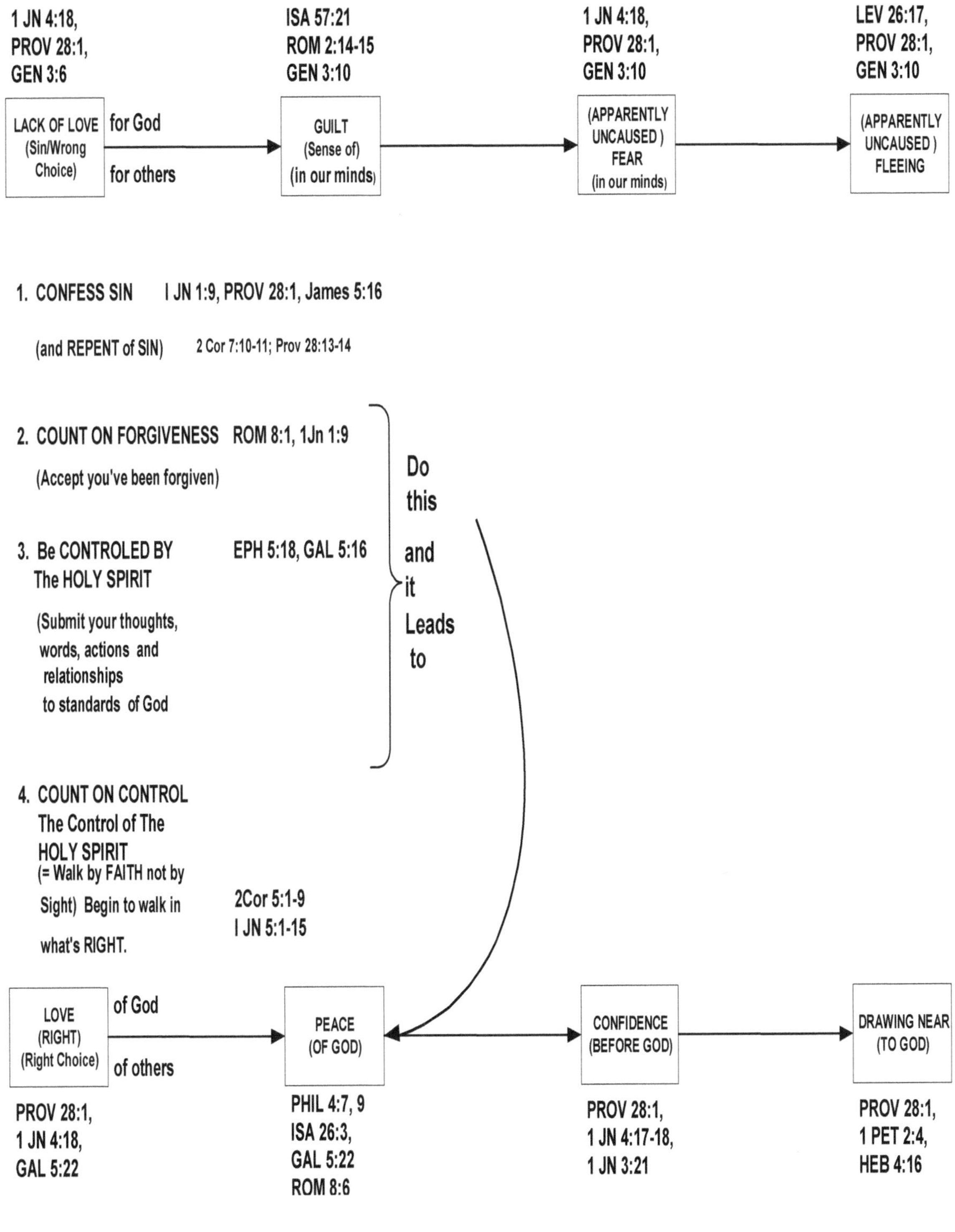

(Concept by Rich Thomson/ this picture of the Framework put together by Greg White)

Section Five

Key Point: *God's Word directly connects the root cause of the immaterial elements of man's mental unsoundness and their physiological effects with his personal responsibility to God.*

(Summary of the Framework)

I. When we make choices that are considered wrong in the sight of God, our conscience produces a sense of guilt leading to a fear a God's judgment and a desire to flee when no one is pursuing.

    A. Sense of Guilt

        1. Knowledge of Guilt (See Romans 7:15-16, 19-20, Psalm 51:3-4, 1 Kings 2:44, Matthew 27:4 and Daniel 9:9-11)

        2. Self-Reproach as result of the knowledge of Guilt (See Isaiah 6:5, Genesis 42:21, 2 Corinthians 7:8-11 and Ezekiel 6:9)

        3. Physical feelings and other results from knowledge of Guilt (See Matthew 26:75, Zechariah 12:10, 2 Kings 22:11

    B. Fear of God's Judgment (Genesis3:10, 4:14, 42:28, Numbers 17:12-13, Psalm 38:18, Acts 24:24-25, Proverbs 28:1, 2 Samuel 6:8-10, Isaiah 33;14, Matthew 27:19, Acts 24:25 and 1 John 4:18)

    C. Fleeing (Genesis 3:10, 4:9, Exodus 32:22-24, Psalm 32:3, Leviticus 26:17, 36-37, Matthew 27:3-5, 1 John 2:28, Romans 1:18-32 and John 3:20-21)

II. When we make choices that are considered right in the sight of God, our conscience vindicates us producing a sense of peace, leading to a confidence before God and a desire to draw near.

    A. Sense of peace (See proverbs 19:23, Colossians 3:15, Philippians 4:7-9, Galatians 5:22, Romans 8:6, Isaiah 26:3, Psalm 119:165)

    B. Confidence before God (See Proverbs 281, 1 John 4:17-18, Psalm 56:9, Proverbs 14:26, 1 John 3:21, 1 John 2:28 and 118:6)

    C. Drawing Near to God (See Proverbs 28:1, Proverbs 18:10, Psalm 63:1a, 6-8, Proverbs 28:5 and John 3:20-21)

III. When a unbeliever has a sense of guilt, apparently uncaused fear or apparently uncaused fleeing and does not submit to Jesus Christ too save him from the penalty of sin, the power of sin and the presence of sin he will seek to:

    A. Do good deeds to cover guilt thus receiving peace that comes from lining up with the work of the law written on his heart not the peace of God (See Romans 2:14-15)

    B. Desensitize his conscience to the guilt of the sin through more sinful thoughts, words and actions thus suppressing the truth in ungodliness and unrighteousness (See Ephesians 4:17-19 and Romans 1:21-23)

    C. Pursue false religions seeking to find in those religions what can only be gained in Jesus Christ alone (See Romans 1:21-23)

    D. Pursue the peace of the world thus receiving a peace that is contingent upon the world's system and temporal pleasures of this life instead of God (See John 1427)
        1. Money
        2. Materials
        3. Medications
        4. Movies
        5. Media
        6. Accomplishments
        7. Human Resources
        8. Entertainment

IV. As a unbeliever does instinctively what is right according to the work of the law written on his heart it will aid in his mental soundness by delivering him from the negative effects of a sense of guilt, apparently uncaused fear and apparently uncaused fleeing until the Holy Spirit convicts him of his sinful condition before a Holy God (See Romans 2:14-15 and John 16:8-11)

V. The peace the unbeliever gets from doing what is right according to the work of the law written on his heart is not the peace of God but the peace of his conscience (See Romans 2:14-15)

VI. The confidence the unbeliever has is based on self-righteousness and the result of lining up with the work on the law written on his heart not God's righteousness produced by faith in Jesus Christ (See Philippians 3:1-6 and Romans 2:14-15)

VII. Unless the Holy Spirit convicts an unbeliever to draw near to accept Jesus Christ he will be drawing near to a false god (See Romans 1:21-23)

VIII. If the unbeliever is not willing to submit to Christ he will seek to find peace through self-righteousness, the world's system/temporal pleasures or false religion (See Philippians 3:1-6, 1 John 315-17, John 1427 and Romans 1:21-23)

IX. There are five kinds of peace:
    A. Peace with God-result of justification (See Romans5:1)

    B. Peace of God-result of making choices that are considered right in the sight of God (See Philippians 4:6-9)

    C. Peace with men-as a result of having a right relationship with God we are to pursue it with men (See Romans 12:18)

    D. Worldly Peace-peace that comes from the world (See John 14:27)

    E. Conscience Peace-peace that is a result of lining up the work of the law written our hearts (See Romans 2:14-15)

X. There are two kinds of confidence:
    A. Confidence in God-trusting God (See Psalm 27:1-3)

    B. Confidence before God-result of making choices that are considered right in the sight of God (See 1 John 4:17-18)

XI. There are two kinds of drawing near:
    A. The results of making choices that are considered right in the sight of God (Psalm 27:1-6)

    B. The result of turning away from sins (See James 4:7-8)

XII. There are many types of fears mentioned in the Bible but there is only one type of fear that results when no one is pursuing or there is no seen danger. That type of fear is the fear of God's Judgment-some psychologists call this anxiety (See Genesis 3:10 and Proverbs 28:1)

XIII. The only fleeing when no one is pursuing is the fleeing from God's Judgment (See Genesis 3:10 and 28:10)

XIV. The ultimate root cause of guilt, fear and fleeing is a lack of love towards God and others (See 1 John 417-18)

XV. The ultimate root cause of peace, confidence and drawing near to God is walking in love towards God and others (See 1 John 4:17-18)

(Insights adapted from <u>The Heart of Man and the Mental Disorders</u> by Rich Thomson)

Key Point: *The absence of God's agape love in man's immaterial heart is the root cause of his guilt and his apparently uncaused fear and fleeing. When there is guilt in the immaterial heart, there is a lack of love towards God and or others. When there is fear in the immaterial heart, there is a lack of love towards God and or others. When there is fleeing in the immaterial heart, there is a lack of love towards God and or others. God's agape love is the basic righteousness produced in man by faith and is the goal of the Word of God in the Christian's life. The lack of God's love is the antithesis of righteousness. Agape Love leads to confidence before God in the Day of Judgment.*

I. *The Correlation of Scriptures Regarding Love*
   A. Matthew 22:37-40—The whole law of God can be summed in loving God and loving others.

   B. Luke 10: 25-28—What Christ was telling the man was impossible for him to do. We cannot love perfectly but as we surrender to Christ we have power thorough the Holy Spirit to do it.

   C. Romans 13:8-10—Love is the fulfillment of the law of God.

   D. Galatians 5:13-14—Love is the fulfillment of the law of God.

   E. James 2:8—Love is the fulfillment of the law of God.

   F. 1 John 4:20-21—One cannot love God without loving his brother; the two go hand in hand.

   G. John 14:15—Loving God is the fulfillment of the commandments.

   H. 1 John 2:10-11—The one who loves his brother abides in the light.

   I. 1 Timothy 1:5—The goal is love which comes from three sources: (1) pure heart, (2) good conscience, and (3) sincere faith. Pure heart and good conscience come from confession of sin and being filled. A real faith brings about a desire to love.

   J. Galatians 5:22—The Spirit of God produces agape love in us.

   K. 1 John 4:17-18—This is the fear of judgment when no one is pursuing; the more fear

   L. I have the less love I have; the more love I have the less fear I have; the specific root wrong is a lack of love; God is love and we should manifest that in our lives.

II. *The Categories of Love*
   A. Eros – love that is based on erotic pleasure; the greater the pleasure one gets from the other person, the greater the love one has for that person; the lesser the pleasure one gets from that person the lesser the love they have for that person; conditioned upon pleasure

B. Stergo – love that is conditioned upon that fact that we have kinship (ex. Brother, Cousin, Uncle etc.); since we are family I treat you okay but if we were not family I would not have any dealings with you; conditioned upon family connection

C. Phileo – love that is based upon affection for the person according to some attraction to them, like interest, common goals or aspirations; the more attraction one feels or pleasure one has or common interest that is developed the more they love the other person; the less attraction one feels or the less pleasure one has with the other person or the less they have in common with the other person they lose love for the other person; conditioned upon attraction and common interest or pleasures

D. Agape – love that is based upon the power of God to seek the highest of good of others unconditionally, no strings attached; it is concerned not with how we feel but how we act. It responds not to the attractiveness of the other person but to the condition and need of the other person. Its motivation is not the selfish desire to enjoy the other person but the selfless desire to benefit him. Essentially, it is concerned and benevolent toward others[1]"

III. The Considerations of Agape Love

A. Agape Love is not something we have to work up to give it's something we work out through the power of the Holy Spirit within us (See Galatians 5:22-23).

B. Agape Love is not a continuum that flows automatically through us; it is developed through practice or derailed through disobedience to God (See 1John 2:9-11).

C. Agape Love is not given according to the character of the receiver but is given according to the character of the giver (See 1John 3:11-24).

D. Agape Love is an unlimited resource from the Nature of God which we can draw from at any time; therefore we have no excuse not love others with agape love (See 1John 4:7).

IV. The Calling to Agape Love

A. We are commanded by God to love Him and to love others with agape love (See Matthew 22:34-40).

---

[1] Boyer *For A World Like Ours.*

B. It is hypocritical to expect agape love from others but not be willing to give agape love to others; we must be willing to give what we ask for (See Luke 6:27-36).

C. Since God is love and we are not the evidence that we are Christians is shown by the agape love that comes through us to others by God (See 1John 4:15-17).

D. We can love others because God loved us (1John 4:19-21).

V. The Characteristics of Agape Love

    A. Agape Love ***is patient***- Love suffers long or able to put up with people, their issues and the issues they bring into our lives for a long period of time and in the proper way without responding in a hastily sinful response internally and externally.

    B. Agape Love ***is kind***- Love is genuine, sincere and willing in attitude as well as genuine and sincere in the actions of ministering good and showing compassion towards others unconditionally for the Glory of God and the blessing of others without looking for anything in return to self from others.

    C. Agape Love ***is not Jealous***- There is not a demeanor of dissatisfaction, rivalry or dislike towards others due to the fact or thought that they are or seem to be, ahead of you, above you, superior to you, or have something you treasure at a level above you. This Love is happy for others in their advancements ahead of you, achievements superior to you, accomplishments above you or acquisitions of things you treasure but do not have or do not have at the level of that person.

    D. Agape Love ***does not brag***- Love does not promote itself, but seeks to promote and to praise God and others above self.

    E. Agape Love ***is not arrogant***- Love does not think of self as more important than others, better than others or the creator and sustainer of all his own abilities, accomplishments, knowledge, blessings, liberties, benefits or experiences. Love has a right view of self, according to one's position before God and position before man with a submissive and servant heart towards God and man as empowered and commanded by God to do so.

F. Agape Love ***does not act unbecomingly***- Love is not rude, rash, impolite, indecent, insensitive, inconsiderate, disrespectful or dishonorable in words, behavior, or actions towards others. Love is considerate, courteous, respectable, right, decent, delicate, sensitive and sympathetic in words, behavior and actions towards others for the glory of God and the benefit of others.

G. Agape Love ***does not seek its' own***- Love does not live to please self. Love lives to please God; thereby, seeking the greatest good of others for God's glory and for other people's utmost welfare.

H. Agape Love ***is not provoked*** – Love is not irritated, not easily annoyed, not easily upset or quick to have a fit in difficult situations with people or in difficult situations in life overall. Love is peaceful in disposition, calm and gentle, in difficult situations with people and in difficult situations in life overall.

I. Agape Love ***does not take into account a wrong suffered*** – Love does not keep a list in one's mind with the intent to get back at others for the sinful, troublesome, painful or disappointing activities of others. Love has a mindset of compassion in relation to the one who has wronged him intentionally, unintentionally, actually or imagined.[2] Love is willing and ready to forgive and forgiving according to God's design.

J. Agape Love ***does not rejoice in unrighteousness but rejoices with the truth***- Love does not take joy in, take pleasure in or find satisfaction in evil or unrighteousness of any kind. Love takes joy in, takes pleasure in and finds satisfaction in right living practiced by others and the triumphs of others in right living practiced.[3]

K. Agape Love ***bears all things***- Love does not give way to the temptation to respond in sin to the pressure put on them by others via their sinful attitudes, strange or unusual ways, or personal preferences. Love seeks to do what is right by others or to others according to the need of the moment on a consistent basis.

---

[2] Rich Thomson, *The Heart of Man and the Mental Disorders: How the Word of God Is Sufficient, a Distinctly Christian Approach* (Alief, Tex.: Biblical Counseling Ministries, 2004), pp. 241.

[3] Wayne A. Mack, *Maximum Impact: Living and Loving for God's Glory* (Phillipsburg, N.J.: P&R Pub., 2010), pp. 205.

L. Agape Love **_believes all things_**- Love seeks to understand people in the best possible light without ignoring or disregarding their proven character flaws and sin issues. Love stays away from developing a suspicious, cynical, doubtful, skeptical, fault-finding, judgmental or hypercritical pattern of thinking about people as a result of their proven character flaws and sin issues.

M. Agape Love **_hopes all things_**- no matter what the situation, love considers the bright side of things for the person by looking to the grace of God in relation to the person.

N. Agape Love **_endures all things_**- Love continues to do what is right with people and in circumstances even when facing difficulty or hardships.

Summary: *Just like a prism displays various colors of light God's love displays various attitudes and actions through the prism of 1Corinthians 13: 4-7. God has made us so that the guilt, fear, and fleeing in our lives push us to grow in love in our lives. The right action with the wrong attitude is bad. The right attitude with the wrong action is bad. Love is defined in both attitude and action. Therefore, we cannot have one without the other and call it love. When people come to you for counseling you will see a lack of love in various areas and be able to help them. One's sufficiency in some areas of love does not make up for the lack of love in other areas.*
(Insights adapted from <u>The Heart of Man and The Mental Disorders</u> by Rich Thomson)

Understanding Anger

I. The *Definition* of Anger (Ephesians 4:26-32)

A. Disposition of the mind that entertains antagonism towards another individual, manifesting itself in various emotions and actions. (Genesis 4:1-8, Mark 3:1-6)

B. Anger is an attitude that results in emotions that move into action.

(Proverbs. 14:17,29,15:18,16:32,19:19,22:24-25)

C. Anger can be godly/righteous indignation- To be troubled or disgusted in attitude or action as a result of someone disgracing God or disregarding His Holy Laws. (Exodus 32:1-30, Ephesians 4: 26-27, John 2:12-17, Nehemiah 5:1-13)

D. Anger can be worldly/sinful of man- to have ungodly attitudes and actions as a result of some perceived need, desire, personal preference /standard not being met by someone or being offended by someone. (Numbers 20:1-13, Ephesians 4:31-32, I Samuel 18:6-8, 20:24-34; James 1:19-20, Matthew 5:21-22)

II. The *Deliberation* on Righteous Indignation Vs. Worldly/Sinful Anger of Man (Ephesians 4:26-32)

A. Godly Anger or Righteous Indignation is the exception to the rule; Very seldom when one is angry it is about the things that disgrace God or disregard His Holy Laws. When one is walking in righteous indignation he/she is filled with desire to see justice done for the glory of God(not self) as he/she is walking by the Spirit of God in this kind of anger. When one does act in Godly anger or righteous indignation he/she is commanded to deal with it before the day is over so that the devil does not use it against him/her to lead him/her into sin.

B. Generally, when people are angry it has nothing to do with someone disgracing God or disregarding His Holy Laws; They are not thinking about God, His holy laws, His righteousness, His will or His ways; They are thinking about themselves, their feelings, their wants, or their needs. They are self-centered not God-centered. They are preoccupied with what they crave, the means to the end that is not providing that craving or something that is hindering that craving from being realized.

C. Therefore, most of the time when people are angry it is generally worldly/ sinful anger of man; what they want within the situation is not granted; They are receiving something they do not want or they are not receiving what they want.

D. As a result of not receiving what they want or getting what they don't want, ungodly attitudes and actions begin to manifest; Instead of being thankful to God for how he will use the situation or accepting what God has allowed in the situation they become negative and ungodly in thoughts, words, actions, and relational patterns.

III. The *Details* of Life that Can lead to Worldly/Sinful Anger of Man

A. Worldly/ sinful anger of man may occur as a result of misplaced dependency- depending on people, place, things, or events to provide what only God provides.

B. Worldly/ sinful anger of man may occur as a result of unrealistic expectations- expecting things that are beyond the scope of possibility.

C. Worldly/sinful anger of man may occur as a result of being untrained in handling disappointments- not accepting the fallibility of people, places, things and events.

D. Worldly/sinful anger of man may occur as a result of not accepting powerlessness over people, places, outcomes of events- resisting the fact that you were not designed to control people and outcome of events.

IV. The *Desires* that become *Demands* of the Heart which is the source of Worldly/Sinful Anger of Man (James 4:1-2)

A. When the desire to be affirmed becomes a demand to be affirmed, worldly/sinful anger of man results when your demands are not met.

B. When the desire to not be put down by others becomes a demand not to be put down by others, worldly/sinful anger of man results when your demands are not met.

C. When the desires that are centered on things of this life become a demand for things of this life, worldly/ sinful anger of man results when your demands are not met:

1. You walk in worldly/sinful anger of man when you demand_____ and do not get it:

   ➢ To have control ,To be loved, To be accepted, To be understood

   ➢ To never hurt again, To be respected, To be served, To have your way

   ➢ To be viewed as competent, To be approved of, To belong to someone

   ➢ To be held in high regard, To maintain a favorable position with people

D. When the desire for people to do or handle things your way or for life to go your way becomes a demand, worldly/ sinful anger of man results when your demands are not met.

V. The *Different* Expressions of Worldly/ Sinful Anger of Man (Ephesians 4:31)

A. Bitterness- resentment.

B. Wrath- intense fury or rage.

C. Anger – deep seated hostility within the heart toward another.

D. Clamor- verbal fighting with people/ Slander- ugly words, mean words in reference to someone's reputation, verbal abuse in reference to someone's character.

VI. The *Dangerous* ways people deal with anger (James 1:19-20, Ephesians 4:26-27)

A. Suppress- acting like it does not exist.

B. Aggression- openly expressed anger at someone else's expense.

C. Passive Aggressive- indirectly expressed anger at someone else's expense.

D. Do not deal with it before the day is done.

VII. The *Direction* to Deal With Anger James 1:19, Ephesians 4:31, Colossians 3:1-8)

A. Acknowledge your anger.

B. Confess the sin of your anger.

C. Identify the details of life whereby you have chosen to be angry.

D. Identify the specific desires you have been demanding to be fulfilled by God, people, places, and events resulting in responding in anger as a result of not getting your way.

E. Accept your inability to control God, people, and the outcome of circumstances

F. Accept these conditions:
   1. The Person may be willing and able.
   2. The Person may be willing and unable.
   3. The Person may be unwilling and able.
   4. The Person may be unwilling and unable.
   5. It may be a desire that was not meant to be satisfied.

G. Accept responsibility for your unloving thoughts, words, deeds, in the situation.

H. Repent of unloving thoughts, words, deeds in the situation.

I. Choose to serve and love others unconditionally.

J. Follow the Biblical Mandate according to the relationship. (1Cor13:4-7)
   1. Husband/Wife (Eph. 5:18-33, Col. 3:18-19, I Peter 3:1-12)
   2. Children (Eph. 6:1-2, Col. 3:20)
   3. Parent (Eph. 6:4, Col. 3:21, Deut. 6:6-9, Prov. 22:6)
   4. Others (I Peter 3:8-12, Rom. 12:9-21, Gal. 6:1-10)
   5. Leaders (I Tim. 4:16, Heb. 13:7, 17;I Peter 5:5, I Tim. 5:17-22, Luke 6:40)
   6. Employer/Employee (Eph. 6:5-9, I Peter 2:18-29)
   7. Government (Rom.13:1-2, I Peter 2:13-17)
   8. Enemies (Luke 6:27-36)

K. Don't allow it to go beyond that day. (Ephesians 4:26-27)

BIBLICAL COUNSELING FRAMEWORK

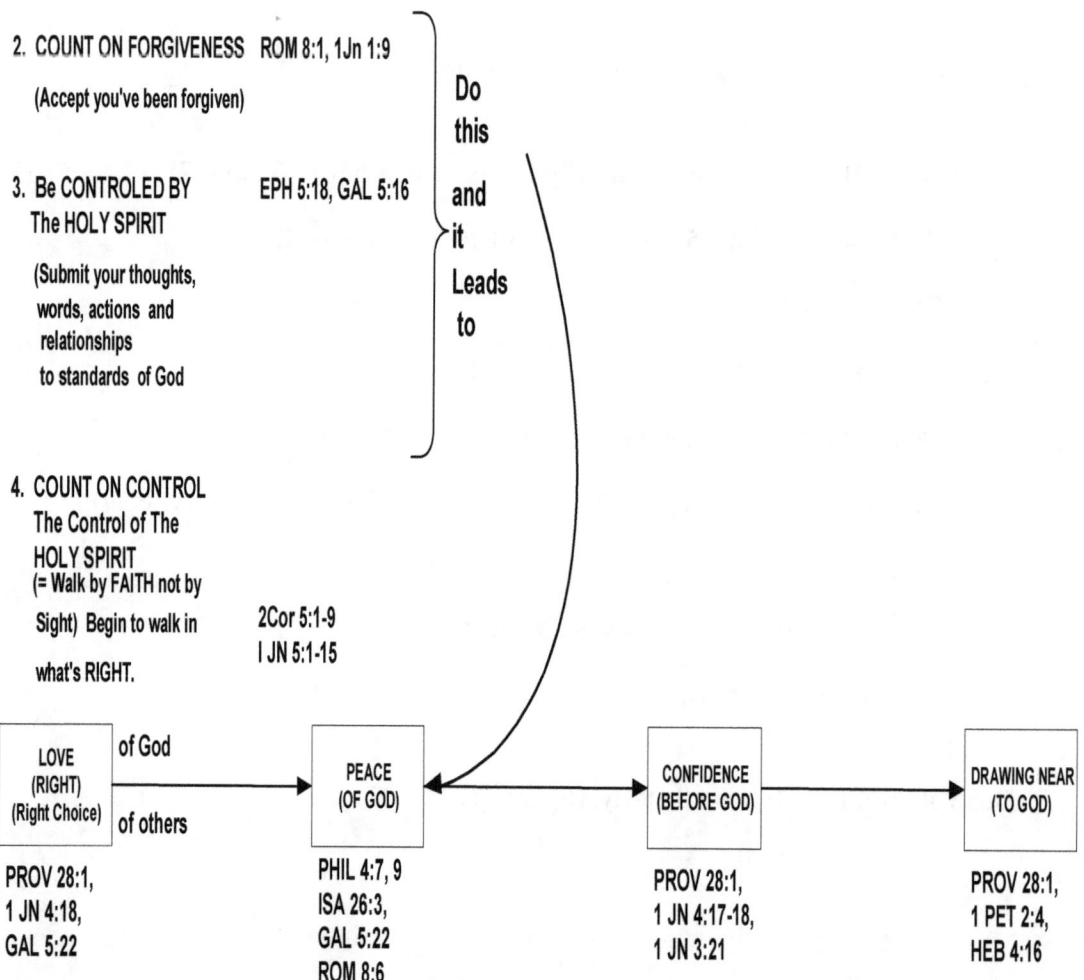

(Concept by Rich Thomson, this picture of the framework put together by Greg White)

Section Six

Key Point: *Since it has been demonstrated that the root of man's mental unsoundness is the lack of God's agape' love (sin) in his heart, the answer to mental unsoundness is first and foremost the confession of sin to God in Jesus Christ and the control of His Holy Spirit Who produces God's love in man's heart. If we confess our sins once a day that is all the filling in the Spirit we get. It needs to be consistent with our sin. As we sin daily we should confess accordingly. As we develop a life pattern of walking in love we will have a life pattern of peace, confidence and a desire to draw near to God. Therefore, expressions of love are the key. Love motivates a person to express. Expressions of love demonstrate the validity of love in our hearts. Expressions of love develop our character and exposes what's in our hearts. If the root answer to problems is love then the main homework assignments given to counselees should be expressions of love.*

I. Though man's heart is always transparent to God who knows all things, man should choose to express to God openly the love which draws him near to God in his heart. In other words, man should have an open loving relationship with God.
   A. Embracing who God is according to His Character/Attributes (See Hebrews 11:6.)
   B. Thinking on good things/Meditating on God's Word (See Philippians 4:8.)
   C. Accepting of what God has allowed in your life (See Romans 8:28 and 1Peter 5:6.)
   D. Entrusting Oneself to God in doing/standing in what is right according to God's will in thoughts, words, behavior or lifestyle (See 1Peter 4:19 and 1Corinthians 16:13-14.)
   E. Thanksgiving for/in all things (See Ephesians 5:20 and 1 Thessalonians 5:18.)
   F. Worship in Spirit and Truth (See John 4:23-24 and Hebrews 10:24-25.)
   G. Praising God Constantly (See Hebrews 13:15, and Psalms 103:1, 150:106.)
   H. Giving to God's Work (See 2 Corinthians 8:3-4, 8; 9:7.)

II. Man should choose to express openly the love which God produces in his heart for his fellow man. In other words man should have open loving relationships with his fellow man. There are four kinds of human relationships: (See Proverbs 27:5-6.)

   A. Sometimes our relationships can be **open and unloving**. (v5)
      1. Rebuking others without respect.
      2. Exposing sin with rudeness.
      3. Exposing character flaws with harshness.
      4. Speaking truth with no love.

B. Sometimes our relationships can be **closed and loving**. (v5)
   1. Appreciative but not expressing it.
   2. Concerned but not showing it.
   3. Having praise in heart but not expressing it.
   4. Desiring the highest good of others but not expressing it.

C. Sometimes our relationships can be **open and loving**. (v6)
   1. Rebuking in love.
   2. Spending quality time.
   3. Speaking the truth in love/giving encouragement.
   4. Meeting needs and bearing burdens.

D. Sometimes our relationships can be **closed and unloving**. (v6)
   1. Talking behind someone's back instead of to them.
   2. Insincere favors or gifts
   3. Flattery
   4. Uncooperative

III. An open loving relationship can be expressed to others in many ways at the right time, in the right way, in the right circumstance through: (See Proverbs 27:14; 25:11; 15:23; 15:1, and Colossians 4:6.)

   A. Sincere apologies (See Matthew 5:23-24 and Romans 12:18.)

   B. Praising others (See Proverbs 27:2, 31:28-29 and 1 Corinthians 11:2.)

   C. Listening and talking to them (See James 1:19 and Proverbs 18:2,13.)

   D. Sharing where you hurt (See 2 Corinthians 6:11-13, 7:2-3.)

   E. Spending time with one another (See 2 Corinthians 12:15, 1 Thessalonians 2:8, Ephesians 6:4, and Titus 2:4-5.)

   F. Gentle correction (See Proverbs 27:6a and 1 Thessalonians 5:14.)

   G. Self-Sacrifice (See 1 Corinthians 13:5 and Philippians 2:3-4.)

H. Submission to God ordained authority (See Ephesians 5:22-6:9, Romans 13:1-7, and Hebrews 13:17.)

I. Saying I love you (See John 13:34.)

J. Giving encouragement (See 1 Thessalonians 5:11, 14, and Proverbs 12:25.)

K. Showing appreciation (See Philippians 4:14)

L. Helping each other (See Acts 20:35 and 1 Thessalonians 5:14.)

M. Comforting each other (See Romans 12:15 and 2 Corinthians 1:3-4.)

N. Bearing one another's burden (See Galatians 6:2.)

O. Warm smile or appropriate touch (See Proverbs 15:30 and Mark 10:13-14.)

P. Phoning or writing expressions of love (See 3 John 1:13-14.)

Q. Asking for help (See Philippians 4:17.)

R. Expressing forgiveness when someone has apologized (See 2 Corinthians 2:7, Ephesians 4:32.)

S. Discipline of one's children (See Ephesians 6:4 and Proverbs 13:24.)

T. Using your spiritual gifts to serve others (See 1 Peter 4:10-11.)

U. Evangelism and Discipleship (See Matthew 28:18-20 and Ephesians 4:11-16.)

IV. When disagreements arise in open loving relationships, unity of heart will be maintained if God's love continues. If unity of heart ceases, apologies should be expressed not for disagreement but for unloving attitudes, words, and actions. You can be right in what you are saying but unloving in your presentation. (Deal with the lack of love.) (See Colossians 3:14, Ephesians 4:15.)

(Insights adapted from <u>The Heart of Man and The Mental Disorders</u> by Rich Thomson)
Ways We Can Embrace God

Characteristics of God to embrace	The Perspective We Should have as a result of embracing this Characteristic?	The Practice we should develop as result of embracing this Characteristic?	The Patterns of relating we should walk in as a result of embracing this Characteristic
Supreme – He is first and foremost before all things; all created things were designed to reflect the greatness of God; His glory is our goal. (Colossians 1:15-19)	I exist for His glory (Romans 11:36}	Live for the audience of God alone, Put God first (1Corinthains 10:31)	Consider God's Glory not your personal gain when relating to others (Philippians 2:1-4)
Sovereign - God controls all things; nothing happens unless God allows it or ordains it; He upholds all things by His power (Ecclesiastes 7:13-14)	My life is in the hands of God and He has it under control (Ecclesiastes 9:1)	Trust God with all your heart by focusing on what you are called to do and stop trying to play God with your circumstances (Proverbs 3: 5-8)	Stop trying to control what others think, say, and do in relation to you or with anything and accept your role under God with them (Matthew 22:34-40)
Sufficient – God is enough and He is doing enough in relation to my life (Psalm 145:17-21)	God is enough and He is doing enough for me (Psalm 73:25-28)	Enjoy what God provides without complaining about what you do not have (Philippians 4:10-14)	Give to others knowing God will supply your needs (Luke 6:30-36)
Holy – unique and set apart from sin while dedicated to His glory (Isaiah 6:1-4)	I must be in the world but be set apart for Christ (1Peter 1:13-16)	Present your body as a living and holy sacrifice to God (Romans 12:1)	Treat others as precious and valuable to God (1Thessalonians 4:1-8)
Loving – seeks the highest good of others; gives himself for the good of others; gives himself to be a blessing to others (Romans 5:8-11)	God is always looking out for me no matter what happens (Hebrews 13:5-6)	Live to be blessing to God (1Corinthians 10:31)	Bear burdens and meet needs of others (Galatians 6:1-2, Titus 3:14)
Wise – He knows and works the best course of action to bring about His greatest glory and our greatest good (Job 9:4-12)	God knows how to bring about the best results for my life (Romans 8:28-39)	Listen to God and follow Him accordingly (Ecclesiastes 5:1-2)	Listen to others with the intent to learn what to do or what not to do accordingly (Proverbs 18:15)
Gracious – showing favor, being a benefit and being generous to people who deserve punishment without them having to earn it or work for it (Ephesians 2:8-10)	I will receive blessings that I don't deserve because of my relationship with God (Psalm 103:1-8)	Give thanks to God and enjoy what He provides (1Thessaloninas 5:18)	Be kind and beneficial to people who don't deserve it (Luke 6:30-36)
Merciful – not giving people the punishment they deserve (2Samuel 24:14-25)	God is always cutting me slack (Psalm 103:9-10)	Repent of all known sin accordingly to God (2Corinthians 7:10-11)	Cut people some slack without dismissing their sin (Romans 12:17-18)
Forgiving – canceled the debt owed by sin; will not hold sin against us (Psalm 103:1-14)	God will always forgive if I ask for it (1John 1:9)	Confess sins to God accordingly (Psalm 32:1-5)	Forgive others as you have been forgiven by God (Matthew 18:21-35)
Faithful – God will always be true to His Word; He will always do whatever He says or promises (Numbers 23:19)	The Lord will never leave me nor forsake me He will always be there (Hebrews 13:5-6)	Serve God faithfully while continuing to wait on His return (1Corinthains 15:58)	Be faithful to others according to the level of the relationship (Proverbs 27:6)

7 Habits of Effective Christians

I cannot accomplish any of these without Christ in my life.

Can I leave any of these out and still be a maturing Christian?

Confession of Sin
1 John 1:9; James 5:16

Repentance of Sin
2 Corinthians 7:10-11; Proverbs 28:13-14

Meditating on God's Word
Romans 12:2; Psalms 1:1-2, 119:11

Forgiving Others as You have Been Forgiven
Ephesians 4:32; Matthew 18:21-35

Applying Truth in Every Aspect of Life
1 Timothy 4:7; 2 Peter 1:1-10

Serving According to Spiritual Gifts
Romans 12:3-8; 1 Peter 4:10-11

Prayer and Worship
John 4:23-23; 1 Thessalonians 5:17

Why don't I practice these more?

Which habit am I focusing on today?

(Concept by Nicolas Ellen picture by Cathy Poulos)

How to Become a Mature Christian

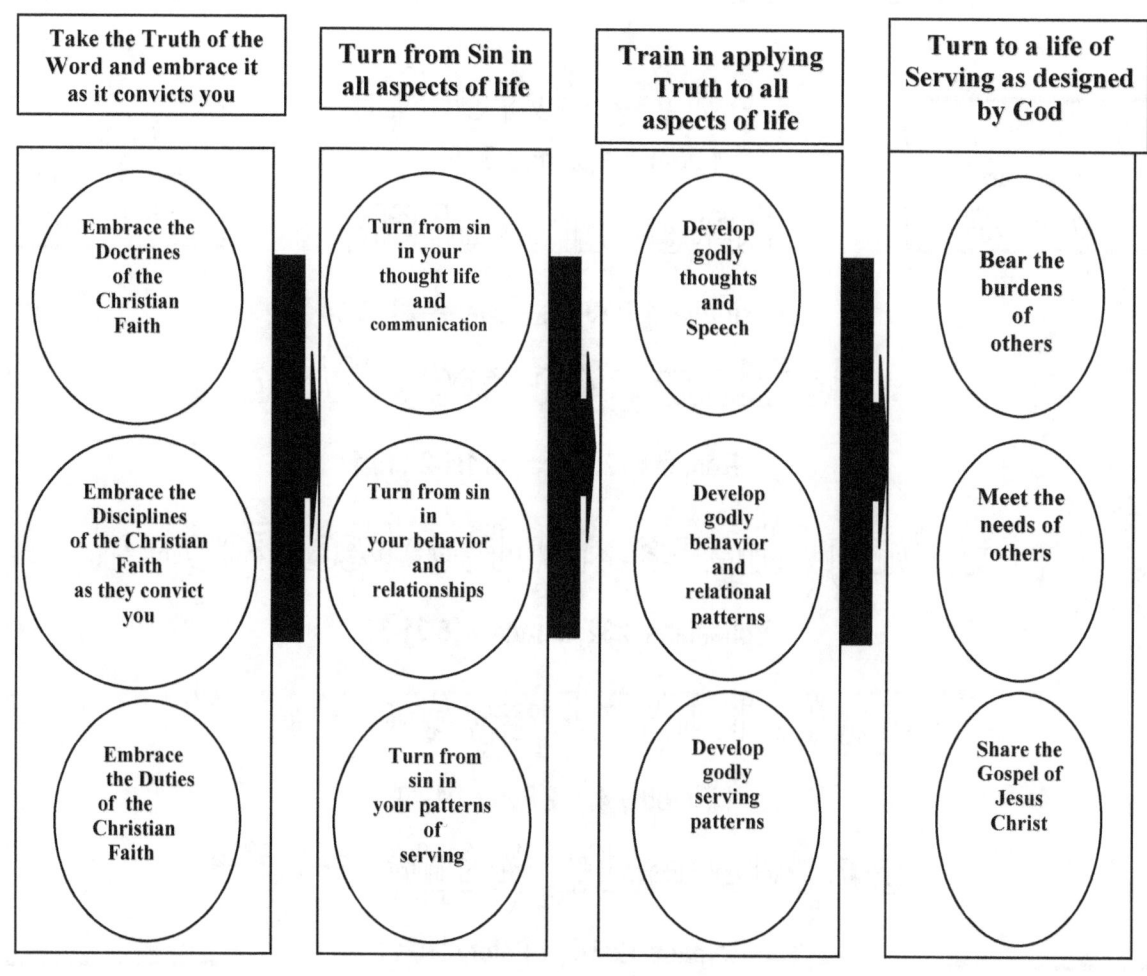

Learning and Living to the Glory of God

Doctrines to Learn	Disciplines to Develop in	Duties to Develop in	Demographics to walk in
God Bible Christ Man Sin Salvation	Confession of Sin Repentance of Sin Meditating on the Word of God	Bearing Burdens Meeting Needs Proclaiming the Gospel	How to be godly in Marriage as a Man as a Woman
Holy Spirit Church Last Things Angels Spiritual Leadership	Forgiving Others Applying Truth Serving Others	Defending the Gospel Giving Monetarily to support the Church	How to be godly as a Senior Citizen as a Young Adult as a College Student
Spiritual Gifts Sanctification Old Testament New Testament Stewardship Judgment Rewards	Prayer/Worship	Corporate Fellowship Corporate Worship	How to be godly as a Teenager as a Child

BIBLICAL COUNSELING FRAMEWORK

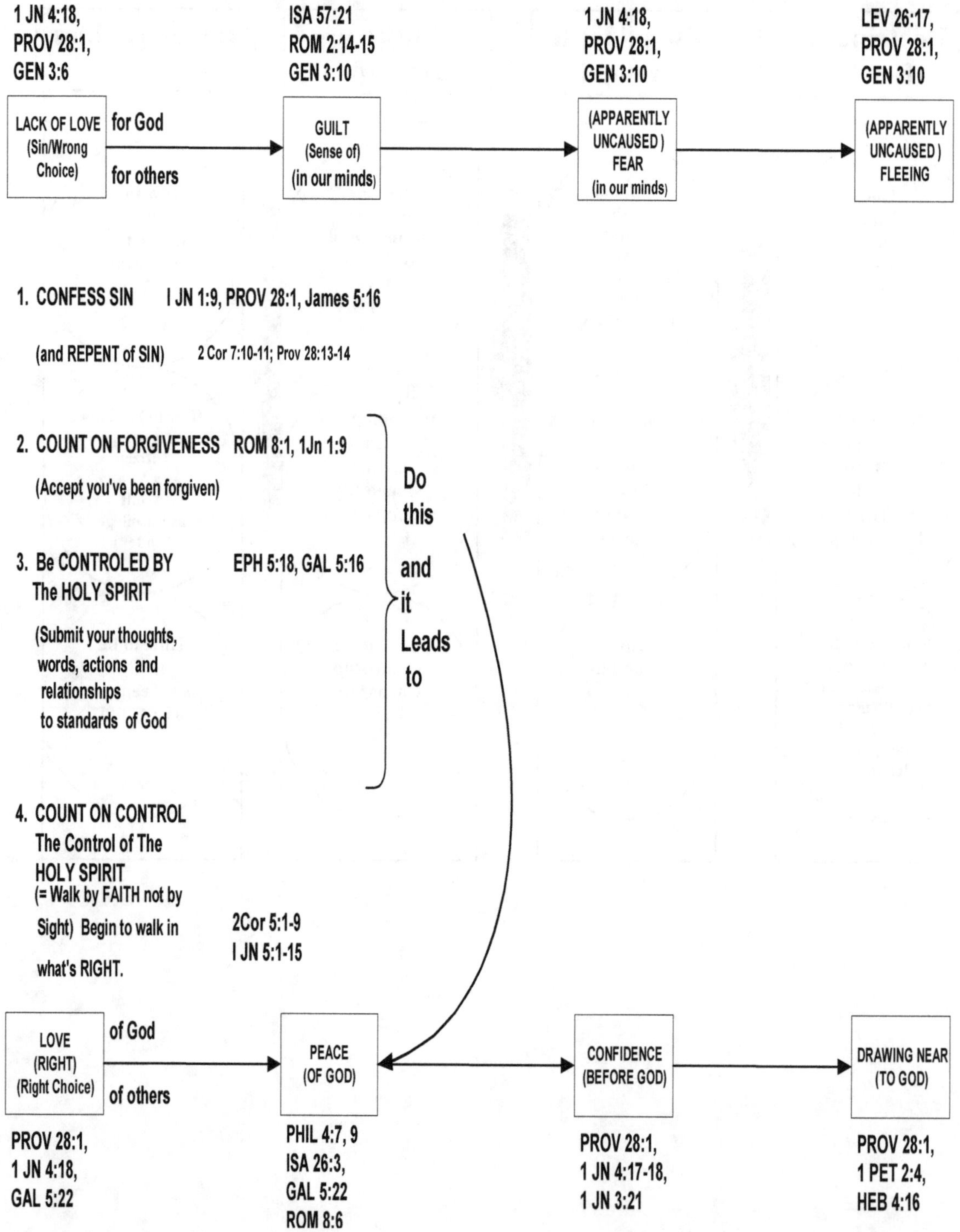

| 1 JN 4:18, PROV 28:1, GEN 3:6 | ISA 57:21, ROM 2:14-15, GEN 3:10 | 1 JN 4:18, PROV 28:1, GEN 3:10 | LEV 26:17, PROV 28:1, GEN 3:10 |

[LACK OF LOVE (Sin/Wrong Choice)] — for God / for others → [GUILT (Sense of) (in our minds)] → [(APPARENTLY UNCAUSED) FEAR (in our minds)] → [(APPARENTLY UNCAUSED) FLEEING]

1. CONFESS SIN   I JN 1:9, PROV 28:1, James 5:16

   (and REPENT of SIN)   2 Cor 7:10-11; Prov 28:13-14

2. COUNT ON FORGIVENESS   ROM 8:1, 1Jn 1:9

   (Accept you've been forgiven)

3. Be CONTROLLED BY   EPH 5:18, GAL 5:16
   The HOLY SPIRIT

   (Submit your thoughts, words, actions and relationships to standards of God)

   { Do this and it Leads to

4. COUNT ON CONTROL
   The Control of The
   HOLY SPIRIT
   (= Walk by FAITH not by Sight) Begin to walk in what's RIGHT.   2Cor 5:1-9
                                                                       I JN 5:1-15

[LOVE (RIGHT) (Right Choice)] — of God / of others → [PEACE (OF GOD)] ↔ [CONFIDENCE (BEFORE GOD)] → [DRAWING NEAR (TO GOD)]

| PROV 28:1, 1 JN 4:18, GAL 5:22 | PHIL 4:7, 9, ISA 26:3, GAL 5:22, ROM 8:6 | PROV 28:1, 1 JN 4:17-18, 1 JN 3:21 | PROV 28:1, 1 PET 2:4, HEB 4:16 |

(Concept by Rich Thomson, this picture of the framework put together by Greg White)

Section Seven

(The Conscience)

Definition of the Conscience: The faculty of the immaterial heart of man that judges the thoughts, intentions, words, and actions of an individual according to the standards given to it by God, human authorities, and personally acquired standards.

I. God's Word reveals that man's conscience is an instinctual judge of his thoughts, words, and actions (See Romans 2:14-15 and Genesis 3:1-7).

   A. The conscience looks at what we think, say and do and makes a value judgment (See Romans 2:14-15).

   B. Man is responsible to God not to violate the dictates of his own conscience (See 1Peter 3:13-16).

   C. The conscience is something all have whether a believer or unbeliever (See Romans 2:14-15).

   D. In the Old Testament it is sometimes expressed through the term "heart" (See 2Samuel 24:10 and Job 27:6).

   E. Here are some other key scriptures to evaluate:
   (1 Samuel 24:5, 2 Samuel 24:10, Romans 14:23, Acts 24:16, Romans 9:1, 1 Corinthians 8:7-13; 10:23-31, 2Corinthians 1:12, 1Timothy 1:5, 19; 3:9, 2 Timothy 1:3, Titus 1:15, Hebrews 9:9, 14; 10:2, 22; 13:18, 1 Peter 2:19, and 1 John 3:21)

II. Man's conscience possesses four sets of standards by which it judges his thoughts, words, and actions. Violation of any of the particulars of any of these four sets of standards is sin against God and renders man unable until confession to love God and others with God's unconditional agape love.

   A. God's Word is a standard of man's conscience—See 1 John 3:21-22, James 4:17.

   B. The work of the law written in the heart (basic understanding of right and wrong)— See Romans 1:32; 2:14-15.

   C. Human Authorities (Governmental regulations, parents, employer, husband, church leader)— See Romans 13:1-7, Ephesians 5&6, Hebrews 13:17.

D. Personally acquired standards (traditions, ideals, gray areas)—See Romans 14:13-23, 1Corinthians 8:1-13, 10:23-31.

III. When we make choices that are considered wrong in the sight of God, our conscience produces:

A. A sense of guilt (knowledge or awareness of wrong)
1. Knowledge of Guilt: (See Romans7:15-16,19-20, Psalm1:3-4,1Kings 2:44,Matthew 27:4, and Daniel 9:9-11.)
2. Self Reproach as result of the knowledge of Guilt (See Isaiah 6:5, Genesis 42:21, 2Corinthians 7:8-11, and Ezekiel 6:9.)
3. Physical feelings and other results from knowledge of Guilt (See Matthew 26:75, Zechariah 12:10, 2Kings 22: 11,19 Psalm 38:1-10, Acts 2:37, Genesis 3:7-8,10-11, Genesis 4:6-7, Luke18:18-23,1John 3:21, and Proverbs 28:1.)

If not confessed and cleared this Sense of Guilt will lead to:

B. A fear of God's Judgment (See Genesis 3:10; 4:14; 42:28, Numbers 17:12-13, Psalm 38:18, Acts 24:24-25, Proverbs 28:1, 2 Samuel 6: 8-10, Isaiah 33:14; Matthew 27:19, Acts 24:25, and 1 John 4:18.)

C. A desire to flee when no one is chasing you (See Genesis 3:10, 4:9, Exodus 32:21-24, Psalm 32:3, Leviticus 26:17, 36-37, Matthew 27:3-5, 1John 2:28, Romans 1:18-32, and John 3:20-21.)

IV. When a unbeliever has a sense of guilt and does not submit to Jesus Christ, he will seek to :

A. Do good deeds to cover guilt. (Romans 2:15)

B. Desensitize his conscience to cover the guilt. (Ephesians 4:17-19)

C. Pursue false religions to cover the guilt. (Romans 1:21-23)

D. Pursue the peace of the world to cover the guilt. (John 14:27)
1. Money
2. Materials
3. Medications
4. Movies,
5. Media
6. Accomplishments
7. Human Resources
8. Entertainment

V. When we make choices that are considered right in the sight of God, our conscience vindicates us producing; a sense of peace, leading to a confidence before God, and a desire to draw near.

A. A sense of peace – tranquility of the heart produced by the conscience and the Holy Spirit for the Believer (See Proverbs 19:23, Colossians 3:15, Philippians 4:7-9, Galatians 5:22, Romans 8:6, Isaiah 26:3, Psalm 119:165)

This sense of peace leads to:

B. A confidence before God (See Proverbs 28:1, 1 John 4:17-18, Psalm 56:9, Proverbs 14:26, John 3:21, 1John 2:28,1Thessalonians 2:2, Psalm 73:24,26; and Psalm 118:6.)

C. A drawing Near to God (See Proverbs 28:1, 1 Peter 2:4, Hebrews 4:16, Psalm 5:11- 12, Daniel 6:10, Proverbs 18:10, Psalm 63:1a, 6-8, Proverbs 28:5, and John 3:20-21.)

VI. As unbelievers submit to the work of the law written in their hearts, or obtain the comforts of the world, they will obtain a peace generated by their conscience or a peace generated by the world only; They cannot gain the peace of God that comes from walking in the righteousness of Christ by faith; they do not belong to God (See Romans 2:14-15, John 14:27, Philippians 4:8-10).

VII. Satan seeks to dull the conscience of the unbeliever so that he may feel happy in his sin and thus be blinded to the truth. The believer has the Holy Spirit to sharpen his conscience making him more sensitive to sin ant the truth. However, we are responsible for how we handle our conscience. Therefore, we must be careful not to weaken our conscience (See 2 Corinthians 4:1-4 and John 16:5-11).

   A. You can numb yourself to the guilt feelings of the conscience enough that you begin to become less sensitive to sin and fleeing when no one is chasing you becomes a way of life (See Ephesians 4:17-19 and 1 Timothy 4:1-2).

   B. You can lose a good conscience by allowing the pressure of outside forces to influence you to bitterness and resentment or by getting a high view of yourself due to your good behavior which are all sin choices that will lead to the conscience producing a sense of guilt thereby causing one to lose a good conscience (See 1Peter 3:16).

   C. You may sin without feeling the guilt, the fear of God's judgment and the desire to flee when no one is chasing due to numbing yourself to the feelings but you will still be aware of the fact the you are guilty of sin (Romans 1:32). However, you cannot have a sense of guilt, the fear of God's judgment and the desire to flee when no one is chasing you without having sin in your life (See Proverbs 28:1 and Genesis 3:1-10).

VIII. According to God's Word all guilt is true guilt before God. Biblically there is no such thing as "false guilt". If you can have a guilt that does not come from sin then you have a guilt that cannot be cleansed or cleared by the blood of Christ, or confession and repentance of sin. Thus, if we have guilt that does not come from sin we have to consult with human wisdom to determine what is true guilt or false guilt since the Bible does not categorize guilt. What people tend to do is to give themselves false reasons for true guilt. There a five key reason why there can be no false guilt:

   A. Practical righteousness before God produces no guilt and no fear of judgment, but known practical unrighteousness produces both guilt and fear. The only biblical exception is the seared or sullied conscience, which may not register the feeling of guilt or a fear of God's judgment even though it will still register the awareness of the fact that one is guilty of sin. However, guilt does not result from righteousness (See Romans 1:28-32, 2:14-15, Proverbs 28:1, 1 John 3:21; 4:18).

B. Man is responsible to God for having a conscience free from guilt (a good conscience).Guilt is therefore an issue between man and God, not a neutral issue which depends upon human wisdom to explain it away as "false guilt". If I am responsible for having a good conscience then I must deal with spiritual issues not neutral issues. Thus my guilt comes from choices I make not through what people have done to me (See 1 Peter 3:16, 1 Timothy 1:19, Hebrews 13:18, Acts 24:16, and 2 Timothy 1:3).

C. Even non moral things (which are not biblically right or wrong) when they are done in violation of one's own conscience are sin against God because they are not result of faith. The guilt incurred is true guilt not false guilt (See Romans 14:22-23 and 1 Corinthians 8 & 9).

D. A believer cannot love with God's love unless he has a good conscience; a conscience free from guilt. To postulate the existence of false guilt which says by definition that one does not have a guiltless conscience means that the believer is dependent on something other than the blood of Christ and confession of sin to rid him of his guilt so that he can love with God's love. Love, however, is dependent upon nothing other than a man's relation with God. It is entirely a spiritual issue (See 1 Timothy 1:5, Galatians 5:22, and 1 John 4:19).

E. The believer is commanded to be filled with the Holy Spirit and to walk by the Spirit. The fruit of the Spirit is peace not guilt. When conviction of the Spirit does produce guilt, it means that the believer is sinning, not walking by the Spirit. If there is a thing such as false guilt, then there are things apart from a right relationship with God that can determine having a good conscience—this is not possible (See Ephesians 5:18, Galatians 5:22, James 2:10, Galatians 5:16, and Isaiah 26:3).

F. Examples and Explanation Where True Guilt Seems to Be False Guilt

1. True guilt may appear to be false guilt when one is giving himself false reasons for his true guilt. For example, the child who feels guilt and blames himself for his father's heart attack is in reality, not paying attention to his true guilt for the anger he has toward God (and maybe toward his father) for allowing the death.

2. True guilt may appear to be false guilt when one thinks he is being "made to feel guilty" by the standards of others, either expressed or unexpressed. Here the true guilt is to be looked for in one of two places. One possibility could be that the one who thinks he is being "made to feel guilty" is accepting in his own heart the standard which is being expected by others which means that He is guilty of violating that personally acquired standard that he has accepted by others which will result in a sense of true guilt in his heart. The second possibility is that one who thinks he is "being made to feel guilty" is experiencing a sense of true guilt as a result of his unloving inner reactions toward those who are attempting to foist upon him standards with which he does not in his heart agree.

3. True guilt may appear to be false guilt when one claims to feel guilty as a result of someone trying to control them through any number of manipulative attitudes, words or actions. In this case, the one who claims to feel guilty as a result of someone trying to control them is experiencing a sense of true guilt because of their unloving attitudes toward the person that is trying to control them.

4. True guilt may appear to be false guilt when one claims to feel guilty about something that is beyond their control. In this case the person is experiencing a sense of true guilt for either walking in the pride of thinking they are in control of the uncontrollable, or for their thankless, un-accepting, or otherwise unloving attitudes towards God who is the great controller, and who "works all things after the counsel of His will."

5. True guilt may appear to be false guilt when one claims to feel guilty because he believes that others do not or will not think well of him for some reason (whether true or not). However, this person is experiencing a sense of true guilt as a result of his unloving inner reactions toward those from whom he believes do not think well of him for some reason (whether true or not).

6. True guilt may appear to be false guilt when one feels guilty about violating a standard that is not in the Bible or some legalistic standards of their own. Here his true guilt before God lies in his violation of his own conscience, not in his violation of any specific moral standard of Scripture. Until such a time as the legalistic standards of his conscience change (hopefully through the education of the Word of God), he should conduct his life by faith according to what his own conscience will or will not allow.

(All the above information was adapted from <u>The Heart of Man and The Mental Disorders</u> by Rich Thomson)

IX. The Bible Exposes Eight Conditions of the Conscience (**All this comes exclusively from The Heart of Man and the Mental Disorders by Rich Thomson**)

   A. The Evil Conscience (Hebrews 10:22)-"a conscience polluted with the guilt of sin," a consciousness of guilt unatoned for and uncleansed away."[4]

   Key Point about the Evil Conscience: The evil conscience is the condition of every conscience before salvation.

   B. The Callous Conscience (Ephesians 4:19) - to cease to feel pain or grief, to become callous, insensible to pain."[5] A conscience that has been deaden to no longer feel its stings. (Even though they are aware of their sin according to Romans 1:32)

   C. The Seared Conscience (1Timothy 4:2) - has been deaden to the point that it has lost all sensitiveness and fails to respond."[6] (Even though they are aware of their sin according to Romans 1:32.)

   Key point about the Callous and Seared Conscience:
   They *know* in their hearts that they are violating God's standards for their lives and that they face judgment for it, but their consciences have been desensitized to the point of being unable to communicate the *pain* of their guilt, unable to stimulate the *fear* of God's judgment, and unable to *move* them to repentance. Their consciences are like that alarm clock which still keeps time and is set for the wake-up call, but whose alarm bell is broken and cannot arouse its sleeping owner.[7]

   D. The Defiled Conscience (Unbeliever) – (Titus 1:15) - to stain, to pollute; consciences polluted to the point at which they are no longer able to sense their guilt or to experience the fear of God's judgment. (even though they are aware of their sin according to Romans 1:32.)

   E. The Defiled Conscience (Believer) – (1Corinthians 8:7) - to stain, to defile, to contaminate; *believers* who are so sensitive to the sin of violating even the non-biblical standards of their own hearts that when they do so, their consciences judge them guilty of sin, and rightly so, "because [their] eating is not from faith, and whatever is not from faith is sin" (Rom. 14:23) (See chapter 10 from The Heart Man and The Mental Disorders.)[8]

---

[4] <u>A Commentary</u>, J,F,B, Vol. III, p. 563
[5] <u>Linguistic Key to the Greek New Testament</u>, p. 533
[6] Lenski, R.C.H., Col, Thess., Tim. ...., Vol. 9, Columbus, Wattburg Press, 1946, p. 621
[7] <u>New Testament Commentary</u>, Hendriksen, Thess. Tim. Tit., p. 146

Key Point about the Defiled conscience in the believer and unbeliever:
The solutions for these two kinds of defiled conscience are very different as well. An unbeliever must come to the Lord Jesus Christ for salvation in order to be cleansed from his evil and from his defilement (Heb. 9:14). A grave problem exists for him, however. Since his defiled conscience almost surely has lost its sensitivity to his sin, it is unlikely that he will be able to sense his need for the Savior. On the other hand, the believer whose conscience is defiled by his sin has no such insensitivity to his guilt. His conscience convicts him of it and, in so doing, urges him towards confession, so that he can receive family forgiveness and the renewed intimacy with God that results from it (I Jn. 1:9, cf. Ps. 32:5, Prov. 28:13).

F. The Good Conscience (Acts 23:1) - one that does not condemn him, not because it is insensitive but because it can detect no faults."

G. The Clear Conscience (1Tim 3:9, 2 Tim 1:3)- "clean, pure, unsoiled…clean from guilt, guiltless, innocent."[9] ; The clear conscience, then, is one which is operating sufficiently (it is not seared or callous) and is not judging one guilty of anything.

H. The Blameless Conscience (Acts 24:16)- a conscience that is "without offense, unharmed, uninjured,"[10] "unblamable, clear."[11]

Key Point about the good, clear, and blameless conscience:
The descriptions good, clear, and blameless are placed together here because they each appear to emphasize various aspects of he same condition of the conscience – a conscience which is free from guilt and judges one's present attitudes, words, and behaviors as acceptable.

X. Summary of the Information on the Conscience:

    A. Man is responsible to God not to violate the dictates of his own conscience. (1Peter 3:13-16)

    B. Violation of his conscience is sin against God and renders man unable until confession, to love God and to love others with God's unconditional agape love. (Romans 14:20-23, 1John 1:1-9)

---

[8] It is also interesting to note that the word defiled in I Corinthians originally meant "'to soil,' 'to smear with dirt'" and "differs from the original sense of the snynon. [used in Titus 1:15]… 'to paint' (Theological Dictionary of the New Testament, Kittel, Vol. IV, p. 644). It would therefore be in keeping with the two different contexts in which these words are found to suggest that the defilement of the unbeliever's conscience is an indelible stain; the defilement of the believer's conscience is a smearing with dirt or a soiling. The second one is washable; the first needs complete bleaching and re-dyeing. (All these notes come from Rich Thomson)
[9] Mounce, p. 257
[10] Linguistic Key to the Greek New Testament, Reinecker Rogers, p. 330
[11] Mounce, p. 96

C. The conscience looks at what we think, say and do and makes a value judgment. (Romans 2:14-15)

D. When the conscience indicates that something is wrong we get a sense of guilt, a fear of God's judgment and a desire to flee when no one is chasing leading to fleeing when no one is chasing. (Genesis 3:6-10)

E. When the conscience indicates that something is right we get a sense of peace, a confidence before God and a desire to draw near to God leading to drawing near to God. A seared or desensitized conscience makes it possible for one to sin and not feel guilt, the fear of God's judgment or the desire to flee when no one is chasing. However, they will still be aware of the fact that they are guilty of sin. (See Proverbs 28:1, 1 John 3:21, 1Timothy 4:2, Ephesians 4:17-19, Romans 1:28-32)

F. The Bible says that we are responsible for our consciousness not our unconsciousness. (1 Peter 3:13-16)

G. The sense of guilt, the fear of God's judgment, and the desire to flee when no one is chasing we experience comes from what the conscience is aware of not what we are not aware of. (Genesis 3: 7-10, Romans 2:14-15)

H. Human wisdom says certain things happen because of our unconsciousness and thus the fear that comes out of nowhere comes out of our unconsciousness. Therefore, we must get back to the past to find out what is wrong with us in order to heal.

I. The Bible shows that the fear that seems to come out of nowhere or what psychologist call the anxiety is the fear of God's judgment which is due to a sense of guilt as a result of a lack of love towards God and or others that is happening in the present not the past. (Genesis 3:6-10)

J. Since we don't choose a sense of guilt or the fear of God's judgment (what psychologist call anxiety), human wisdom tries to say it comes from our unconsciousness.

K. On the other hand, the Bible shows that it is the result of sinful choices and comes from our conscience which produces a sense of guilt and a fear of God's judgment, which results in our desire to flee when no one is chasing leading to fleeing when no one is chasing. (See Genesis 3:6-10, Proverbs 28:1, Romans 2:14-15.)

L. It's not what happened in my past that brings about a sense of guilt, a fear of God's judgment, fleeing when no one is chasing, a sense of peace, confidence before God, drawing near but my present loving or unloving attitude towards the past that brings about these various by-products.

M. The conscience is never wrong, but it is not always right.

N. That is the conscience is never wrong when it convicts man of sin.

O. But it is not always right when it exonerates man of guilt (1Corinthians 4:4).

P. Several reasons have been given to establish that when man is aware of guilt in his conscience, it is true guilt before God.

Q. There may be many and varied expressions of what appear to be false guilt, but once one understands that Scripture is clear that all guilt is true guilt, it is not difficult to find this true guilt in the relationships and situations which accompany its presence. Then, as the root sins are confessed and as the Holy Spirit produces His love within the heart, the results will be a sense of peace, confidence before God and a desire to draw near to God leading to the action to draw near to God and to others.

Questions to Consider:

1. If you were to evaluate your life how much guilt do you tend to encounter on daily/weekly basis?

2. How have you been dealing with this guilt on daily/weekly basis?

3. Prior to reading this material what has been your view of guilt?

4. What has this information challenged you to consider about guilt?

5. Based upon what you have read what would you say is the source of your guilt?

6. Based upon what you have read what standard of the conscience have you violated?

7. Have you given yourself false reasons for true guilt? If so explain where that has taken place in your life.

8. What are the real reasons for your true guilt in the context of the situation? What steps will you take to address it accordingly?

Section Eight
Emotions
(Insights taken from the Book <u>The Heart of Man and Mental Disorders</u> by Rich Thomson)

Definition of Emotion: The word originated from the Latin *emovere* (*e-,* out plus *movere,* move); It means to "stir up." Stirrings that move one to action or decision.

- I. **The World's View of Emotions**: The world sees emotions as a product of man's evolutionary history. Simply put, man is merely a highly evolved animal who has the same emotions as other animals.

- II. **The Biblical View of Emotions**: God is Spirit (Jn. 4:24) and has no physical brain or body. In His very nature He possesses qualities which are consistently regarded by human wisdom as emotions. Examples: Love (I Jn. 4:8, 16), Jealousy (Nahum 1:2), Anger (Hebrews 3:10), Hatred (Ps. 5:5), Joy (I Tim. 1:11), Sorrow (Eph. 4:30). Not only does God possess emotions apart from a material existence, His Word also teaches that He has created mankind in His own image (Gen. 1:26) with an immaterial aspect to his nature in which he too, experiences emotion. Examples: Godly/Sinful hatred (Ps. 105:25, Lev. 19:17), Anger (Eccl. 7:9, 11:10), Envy (Prov. 23:17), Fear (Jn. 14:27, Deut. 28:17, Isa. 35:4), Joy (Ps. 13:5, Jn. 16:22), Sorrow (Jn. 16:6, Rom. 9:2).

- III. **God's Judgment of Emotions**: Emotions of animals originate in their brains and bodies and they have no immaterial nature in which they are responsible to God. Mankind, on the other hand, has an immaterial nature, and according to Scripture, most of his emotions originate in that nature. God weighs as right or wrong those moral attitudes in man's life which determine the emotions. God does not judge the experience of the emotions themselves as right or wrong, but He does weigh the heart attitudes which initiate them (I Cor. 4:5, Prov. 21:2, I Chron. 28:9, Jer. 17:10, cf. Heb. 4:12).

IV. **The Three Areas where Emotions Originate:** *1. Attitude* – Human emotions originate as a thought or a system of thoughts in one's immaterial heart which then are experienced as emotions in his immaterial heart, physical brain and physical body. Examples: Grief (Matthew 26:36-38), Disappointment (Proverbs 13:12), Agony (Luke 22:44) 2. *Conscience* – Human emotions originate as thoughts of warnings or affirmations of the conscience upon man's right or wrong attitudes, words, and actions. The conscience excuses, or accuses man (Romans 2:14-15) which in turn, stimulates the emotions he experiences in his immaterial heart, physical brain, and physical body from the excusing and accusing of the conscience. Examples: Bothered (1Samuel 24:5), Troubled (2Samuel 24:10), Confidence (1John 3:21). **3.** *Physiological Emotion* – Human emotions originate in man's material brain as thoughts of warnings of possible physical danger, or thoughts of pain or pleasure being experienced as an emotion in the body. Examples: Startle or Fright (Ruth 3:8), Pleasure (Proverbs 21:17), Affliction (2Corinthians 4:8).

Emotions

> God's is Spirit; He has emotions; We are created in His image

⬇

> **Since we are created in His image our emotions mainly come from our immaterial heart**

⬇

> *Our Thoughts/attitudes determine what we feel; they determine our emotions*

⬇

> *Therefore, my emotions are a by-product of my thoughts/attitudes*

⬇

> *There are three areas where these emotions derive:*
> *A. The mind of man produces attitudes which produce emotions*
> *B. The conscience of man produces attitudes (your right or your wrong) which produce emotions*
> *C. The brain produces warning resulting in the emotions of startle or fright as well as pleasure and pain*

Emotions

> **Since Emotions come from your immaterial heart:**

⬇

> There is no such thing as damaged emotions because emotions are the window to the thoughts and attitudes of our hearts.

⬇

> **We cannot be emotionally abused by others because our emotions/feelings are a by-product of what we are thinking. We decide what we will think which determines our emotions/feelings**

⬇

> *We control our emotions by controlling our thoughts/attitudes because emotions come from what we are thinking. If we control our thinking we control our emotions/feelings*

⬇

> *No one can determine what we feel because our feelings/emotions come from our thoughts/attitudes. Therefore, no one hurts your feelings. Your have feelings/emotions of hurt because of what you are thinking about the person who disappointed you or sinned against you.*
>
> *As a result, you cannot blame anyone for your feelings/emotions. The way you choose to think determines the way you feel or the emotions you have.*

Examples of Each of These Kinds of Emotions:

I. Attitude Emotions

A. Neutral Attitude Emotions:

common joy, common sorrow, amusement, delight, ecstasy, elation, enjoyment, euphoria, happiness, grief, anguish of heart, discomfort, displeasure, distress (when distress simply means troubled, not hopelessness), loneliness(when the reference is to one's relationship with other people), sadness, sorrow, uneasiness, unhappiness, embarrassment, regret

B. Moral Attitude Emotions:

benevolence, contentment, empathy, gratitude, love, pity, and sympathy, aggression, agitation(where it does not simply mean physical discomfort) anger, annoyance, fury, hate, hostility, irritation, rage, vexation, anxiety, apprehension, distress (when this means worry), dread, fear, terror, worry, dejection, depression, distress (not physically referenced), gloom, hopelessness,[12] envy, jealousy, contempt, pride, querulousness ,self-pity, ungrateful, thanklessness, passivity, submission, confidence

C. Situational Moral Attitude Emotions:

Neutral attitude emotions that are used in a loving or unloving way- taking *pleasure* in wickedness, *rejoicing* in the suffering of the wicked, rejoicing in the repentance of sin, grief over not being able to sin as you want

II. Conscience Emotions

A. Sense of guilt, the sense of apparently-uncaused fear (fear of judgment), the sense of peace, the sense of confidence before God, bothered conscience, troubled conscience

III. Physiological Emotions

A. Startled, frightened, bodily pain, bodily pleasure

---

[12] Hopelessness is not only a Moral Attitude-Emotion but, interestingly, is also a Conscience-Stimulated Attitude-Emotion (discussed later).

Joy and Sorrow

(Adapted from The Heart and Man and The Mental Disorders by Rich Thomson)

Categories of Joy

A. **Common Joy**—joy that happens as a result encountering good things, or encountering positive circumstances or people; it is neither right nor wrong to experience this joy; it is neutral and experienced by all (See Acts 12:14).

B. **Conscience Joy**—joy that happens when you make morally right choices; the conscience produces this kind of joy (See Romans 2:14-15).

C. **Chosen Joy**—a choice to be joyful no matter the circumstance (See Philippians 4:4).

  1. Right Chosen Joy:
     a. One can be joyful over the execution of justice (See Proverbs 21:15).
     b. One can think on good things (See Philippians 4:8).
     c. One can rejoice in the Lord (See Philippians 4:4).
     d. One can count it all joy in trials (See James 1:2).
     e. One can give thanks for all things (See 1Thessalonians 5:18).

  2. Wrong Chosen Joy:
     a. One should not rejoice when his enemy falls (See Proverbs 24:17).
     b. One should not rejoice in sin (See Proverbs 15:21, and 1Cor. 13:6).
     c. One should not rejoice in a negative way over the death of Christ (See John 16:20).

Understanding the Kinds of Sorrow Mentioned in the Bible

I. *Common* Sorrow (Proverbs 13:12, Roman 12:15, John 11:1-44) – a sadness of the soul due to one experiencing the disappointments of life, the difficulties of life, or the death of a loved one. For example:

A. One has a sadness of heart as a result of unmet expectations yet there is no corresponding sin with that sadness.

B. One has a sadness of heart as a result of experiencing tragedy in their lives or being mistreated by others, yet there is no corresponding sin with that sadness.

C. One has a sadness of heart as a result of experiencing the death of someone they were attached to yet there is no corresponding sin with that sadness.

II. *Chosen* Sorrow (Philippians 2:14-15, 1Thessalonians 5:15) – a sadness of the soul created by one grumbling or complaining about their circumstances. For example:

A. One does not like and is unwilling to accept what God has allowed in the circumstances, so one complains about it creating a sadness of soul.

B. One is unwilling to accept that people are not operating as they would like them to, so one complains about it creating a sadness of soul.

C. One is unwilling to accept the difficulties in life, so one complains about it creating sadness of soul.

III. *Conscience* Sorrow (Romans 2:14-15, 1Samuel 24:1-5, 2Samuel 24:10)- a sadness of soul as a result one's conscience bringing about guilt due to some act(s) of sin in one's life. For example:

A. One has been thinking in a sinful manner resulting in the conscience bringing about guilt in one's heart leading to a sadness of soul.

B. One has been talking in a sinful manner resulting in the conscience bringing about guilt in one's heart leading to a sadness of soul.

C. One has been living in a sinful manner resulting in the conscience bringing about guilt in one's heart leading to a sadness of soul.

IV. *Casualty* **Sorrow (Genesis 4:1-14, 2Corinthians 7:10)**- a sadness of soul as result of regret over the consequences of sin choices ultimately leading one to death because of a lack of repentance. For example:

   A. One is sorrowful about what is going to happen to him/her as a result of the sin.

   B. One is not focused on how their sin has dishonored God or damaged others.

   C. Since there is no change of heart only grief about the issue, one experiences more complications, problems, pain and ultimately death because of the consequences of a continued life of sin.

V. *Contrite* **Sorrow (2 Corinthians 7:10-11, Luke 18:9-14)** - a sadness of soul because one is broken over their sin against God. For example:

   A. One is grieved over how their sin has dishonored God.

   B. One is grieved over how they have brought sorrow to God because of their sin.

   C. As a result of grief over sin against God, one is wanting and moving towards making things right with God according to God's will and ways.

VI. *Chastisement* **Sorrow (Hebrews 12:11)** – a sadness of soul because one is experiencing the discipline of God leading to a product of righteousness in their living. For example:

   A. One is grieved as they experience the discipline of God producing righteousness in their thoughts, desires, and motives.

   B. One is grieved as they experience the discipline of God producing righteousness in their communication, behavior, manner of life or manner of serving.

   C. One is grieved as they experience the discipline of God producing righteousness in their relationship patterns.

Section Nine

Distinguishing Between the Various Types of Fears Mentioned in the Bible

I. The Bible mentions a kind of fear that is not sinful. It is neutral. It is a fear which has a definite ***external cause***. It can be traced to something specific externally.

    A. Startle or fright - an instantaneous and instinctual response to possible bodily danger. (Ruth 3:8, Luke 24:37)

II. The Bible mentions another set a fears which are good and right. These kinds of fears have a definite ***external cause***. They can be traced to something specific externally. These kinds of fears are consistent with loving and trusting God.

    A. Fear that is described as ***reverence*** for the Lord is consistent with loving and trusting God. (Proverbs 1:7)

    B. Fear that is described as ***concern*** is consistent with loving and trusting God. (Galatians 4:11)

    C. Fear that is described as ***respect*** is consistent with loving and trusting God. (Romans 13:7, 1 Peter 3:2)

III. The Bible mentions another set of fears which are wrong and sinful. These kinds of fears have a definite ***external cause***. They can be traced to something specific externally. These fears are inconsistent with loving and trusting God.

    A. Having a fear of ***false gods*** is inconsistent with loving and trusting God (Jeremiah 10:2-5)

    B. Being ***worried*** is a fear that is inconsistent with loving and trusting God (Luke 12:4-7, 32)

    C. Being timid, cowardly, or ***intimidated*** is a fear that is inconsistent with loving and trusting God (2 Timothy 1:7, Joshua 1:9, Proverbs 29:25)

IV. The Bible mentions another kind of fear which is the by-product of internal guilt. It does not have a discernable **_external cause_**. It is traced solely to **_internal guilt_**. It is called the fear of God's **_judgment._** This is commonly known and called anxiety. Psychologists define anxiety as a fear which has no discernable external cause. They observe that is comes and goes for no external reason. There is no external apparent cause because it is a by- product of a guilty conscience, yet they would deny this reality.

    A. The fear of God's **_judgment_** is seen in Adam when he sinned; it was not caused by anything external; It was a by-product of his guilty conscience which was the result of his sin choice (Genesis 3:1-10).

    B. The fear of God's **_judgment_** is seen when people are running and no one is chasing them. The fear is not caused by anything external; it is a by-product of a guilty conscience which is the result of making a sin choice (Proverbs 28:1, Leviticus 26:17, 36-37).

    C. The fear of God's **_judgment_** is not like any of the other fears because it is not something we control by choice it is the by-product of a choice. We don't deal with the fear of God's judgment through actually dealing with the fear (or what psychologists call anxiety). We deal with it through confessing our sins. (Psalm 32:1-5, Proverbs 28:13)

Insights and concepts adapted from The Heart of Man and The Mental Disorders by Rich Thomson)

The Fear of Worry vs. The Fear of God's Judgment (Anxiety)
(Concept adapted from Rich Thomson)

The Fear of Worry	The Fear of God's Judgment (Anxiety)
The Fear is attached to a visible issue.	The Fear is not attached to a visible issue.
The Fear is in proportion to the threat.	The Fear is out of proportion to the threat.
The root of the problem is not trusting God with the issues.	The root of problem involves an unloving attitude, word or actions and the person is unable to see that it is producing the fear that seems to come out of nowhere.
Counseling focuses on trusting God with the thing the person is fearful about.	Counseling focuses on finding the root unloving attitude, word, or action that is producing the fear that seems to come out of nowhere so that they may confess, count on forgiveness, be controlled by the Holy Spirit and count on the control of the Holy Spirit as they walk in love in that area which help them overcome the fear that seems to come out of nowhere.
The Fear comes and goes as troubles come and go.	The Fear hangs on whether troubles are present or not; It's difficult to even understand why is disappears when it does.
One should confess his fear as sin.	One should identify the sin that is producing the fear that seems to come out nowhere because the fear is the result of that sin not sin itself.

Expressions

Key Point: Below is a list of ways in which a lack of love, guilt, uncaused fear, and uncaused fleeing tend to be expressed or demonstrated in everyday life situations. As we continue in our studies we will begin to use this terminology to explain how a lack of love, guilt, uncaused fear, and uncaused fleeing is being demonstrated in a person's life or in some case we will study. For instance we may say something such as:

    a. That is an expression(demonstration) of uncaused fleeing

    b. That is an expression(demonstration) of uncaused fear

    c. That is an expression (demonstration) of a sense of guilt

    d. That is an expression(demonstration) of a lack of love for God or others

This means that one of the elements of the framework is being expressed or demonstrated.

1. Lack of Love Expressions (Ways in which a lack of love may be expressed or demonstrated in everyday situations):

    A. Impatience, irritability, annoyance, anger, rage, cruelty, unkindness, jealousy, envy, enmity, hostility, hatred, bragging, pride, conceit, immorality, impurity, indecency, criminality, thoughtlessness, greed, selfishness, stubbornness, obstinacy, self-centeredness, grumbling, thanklessness, discontentment, resentment, grudge-bearing, un-forgiveness, bitterness, maliciousness, suspicion, pessimism, hopelessness

2. Guilt Expressions (Ways in which a sense of guilt may be expressed or demonstrated in everyday situations):

    A. Feeling guilty, sense of condemnation, anticipation of punishment, bothered conscience, accusing thoughts, down on self, low self-respect, sense of worthlessness, self-condemnation, excessive doubt about doing something

3. Uncaused Fear Expressions (Ways in which uncaused fear may be expressed in everyday situations):

A. Anxiety, uneasiness, apprehension, dread, tension, restlessness, excessive worry, anticipation of misfortune, danger or doom, irritability, over dependence, timidity, shyness, panic, terror, over concern, hyper-happiness, imagination of illness, agitation, over-activity, easy distraction, persecution complex.

B. *When uncaused fear continues it may begin to affect the body. As a result one may begin to experience some physiological effects on the body because one is not dealing with their sin (Psalm 32:1-5). Some things which may be the physiological effects of uncaused fear are:*

   a. Hyper-alert, fidgety, talking to much, falling asleep, impaired concentration, poor memory, excessive perspiration, muscle tension, headaches, sighing respirations, hyperventilation, abdominal pain, nausea, diarrhea, butterflies, high blood pressure, rapid heartbeat, fainting episodes, frequent urination, impotence, frigidity, ulcers, nervous stomach, depletion of brain chemicals, hormone irregularities, weakened immune system

4. Uncaused Fleeing Expressions (Ways in which uncaused fleeing may be expressed in everyday situations):

A. Withdrawal, isolation, escape, inner hiding, denial, defensiveness, excessive self-protection, abandonment or denial of self- evident truth, escape from reality, withdrawal of intimacy, embracing of fantasy as reality, pursuit of imaginary states, desperation to flood one's mind with stimuli, desperation to flood one's body with stimuli, anesthetizing one's brain, unwillingness to be open, living in a fantasy world, unwillingness to reason, delusions, blaming, self-justification, changing the subject, trying to get rid of another person, (criticizing others about their sin while denying that same sin in ourselves, trying to live properly without dealing with our sin/ these concepts from David Powlison)

(Expression derived from Minrith, Meier, and Rich Thomson, David Powlison)

Biblical Diagnosis

A husband and wife are having a discussion. They don't seem to agree on a issue. There seems to be a pattern that every time the husband and wife don't agree the husband withdraws.

1. What expression is he demonstrating?

2. What is the root cause of this expression he is demonstrating?

3. How did you come to this conclusion?

Using the Biblical Framework we have been studying and the expressions sheet we have been studying:

A. Diagnose what these following problems seem to be an expression of according to the biblical framework and give a Scripture to support your answer.

B. Diagnose what the root causes of the following problems are according to the biblical framework.

C. Explain why you have come to your conclusion

1. Anxiety Disorder
    A. Anxiety Disorder is an expression of_____

    B. The Scripture to support this is_____

    C. The root cause of anxiety disorder is _____

    D. I have come to this conclusion because:

2. Alcoholism
    A. Alcoholism is an expression of_____

    B. The Scripture to support this is_____

    C. The root cause of alcoholism is _____

    D. I have come to this conclusion because:

3. Not talking to each other (withdrawing from each other)

    A. Not talking to each other is an expression of_____

    B. The Scripture to support this is_____

    C. The root cause of not talking to each other is _____

    D. I have come to this conclusion because:

4. Multiple Personalities

    A. Multiple Personalities is an expression of_____

    B. The Scripture to support this is_____

    C. The root cause of multiple personalities is _____

    D. I have come to this conclusion because:

5. Panic Disorder

    A. Panic Disorder is an expression of_____

    B. The Scripture to support this is_____

    C. The root cause of panic disorder is _____

    D. I have come to this conclusion because:

6. Drug Abuse

    A. Drug Abuse is an expression of_____

    B. The Scripture to support this is_____

    C. The root cause of drug abuse is _____

    D. I have come to this conclusion because:

7. **Suicide Ideation**

    A. Suicide Ideation is an expression of_____

    B. The Scripture to support this is_____

    C. The root cause of suicide ideation is _____

    D. I have come to this conclusion because:

(Idea for activity above is from Rich Thomson)

There are five areas where we can look to find the lack of love expressions that are producing the various expressions uncaused fleeing, uncaused fleeing and a sense of guilt we see everyday life situations:

1. Thought/Attitudes/Belief System, intentions/motives, desires

2. Communication

3. Behavior and Lifestyle

4. Relational Patterns

5. Service or lack thereof towards God and others

When lack of love is being expressed towards God and others, you will find it is being expressed in any one of these areas of a person's life.

Section Ten

Self Esteem, Self Image, Self Love

Key Points About Self Esteem

I. Understanding the Conscience
   A. The conscience can be defined as the faculty of the immaterial heart that judges the thoughts, intentions, words, and deeds of an individual according to the standards given it by God, governing authorities, personally acquired standards (See Romans 1:18-20,32, Romans 2:14-15, Romans 13:1-5, and Romans 14: 22-23).
   B. Man's conscience is an instinctual judge of his thoughts, words, and actions accusing him when he does something that is morally wrong and excusing him when he does something that is morally right (See Romans 2:14-15).
   C. The conscience is a universal entity in that all have it whether believer or unbeliever (See Romans 1:18-20, Romans 2:14-15, and 1Timothy 3:8-9).

II. Understanding Conscience Joy and Conscience Sorrow
   A. When a person makes a choice that is morally right their conscience will produce a joy resulting in one having a satisfaction with himself (See Genesis 4:1-7).
   B. When a person a makes a choice that is morally wrong their conscience will produce a sorrow resulting in one having a sense of dissatisfaction with himself (See Genesis 4:1-7).
   C. This sense of satisfaction and dissatisfaction with oneself is where we see the concept of self-esteem coming together.

III. Definition of Positive and Negative Self Esteem
   A. Definition of Positive Self-Esteem: satisfaction with one's self, self respect, sense of assurance (conscience joy).
   B. Definition of Negative Self-Esteem: dissatisfaction with one's self, low self respect, sense of insecurity (conscience sorrow).
   C. They are the by-product of right and wrong choices.

IV. Positive self-esteem is a by-product of doing what is right (See Genesis 4:6-7).

    A. Positive self-esteem is characterized by a clear conscience—peace (See Romans 2:14-15).

    B. Positive self-esteem is characterized by confidence from within the heart (See Proverbs 28:1).

    C. When one responds in the right way to any and all types of circumstances it will produce positive self esteem (conscience joy) which is produced at the root by the work of the conscience (See 1John 3:21).

V. Negative self-esteem is a by-product of living in sin (See Genesis 4:6-7).

    A. Negative self-esteem is characterized by a guilty conscience (See Romans 2:14-15).

    B. Negative self esteem is characterized by fearfulness within the heart (See Proverbs 28:1).

    C. When one responds in the wrong way to any and all circumstances it will produce negative self-esteem (conscience sorrow) which is produced at root by the work of the conscience (See 1 Samuel 24:1-7).

VI. When a unbeliever has positive self-esteem it is the by-product of appeasing the work of the law written in his heart—*Conscience Joy* (See Romans 2:14-15).

    A. As a non-believer lines up to the dictates of his conscience it will aid in his mental soundness by delivering him from the negative affects of a sense of guilt until the Holy Spirit convicts him of his sinful condition before a Holy God (See Romans 2:15 and John 16:8-11).

    B. The peace the non-believer gets from lining up with his conscience is what we call conscience joy which is universally experience by believer and unbeliever (See Romans 2:15 and Proverb 28:1).

    C. This is why positive self-esteem occurs in an unbeliever—Conscience Joy (See Romans 2:14-15).

VII. In the worst case, when an unbeliever has positive self-esteem, it is the by-product of searing or numbing his conscience to the sense of guilt and the conscience sorrow (negative self-esteem) that results (Romans 1:28-32, Ephesians 4:17-19, Romans 2:14-15, John 14:27).

   A. As a non-believer sears or numbs his conscience, he no longer feels the conscience sorrow/ negative - self esteem that results from a guilty conscience even though he is aware of his guilt before God. (Romans 1:32, Ephesians 4:17-19, 1Timohty 4:1-2)

   B. The non- believer experiences joy as a result of doing something right (conscience joy/ positive self- esteem) but not sorrow that comes from wrong doing because he has numbed or seared his conscience to the feelings of guilt that bring the conscience sorrow/ negative self- esteem. He is aware of the guilt before God but is not experiencing the conscience sorrow/ negative self-esteem with the awareness. (Romans 2:14-15, Ephesians 4:17-19, Romans 1:28-32, 1Timothy 4:1-2)

   C. The non -believer experiences the peace that world gives but not the sorrow that comes from wrong doing because he has numbed or seared his conscience to the feelings of guilt that bring the conscience sorrow/negative self-esteem. He is aware of the guilt before God but is not experiencing the conscience sorrow/ negative self-esteem with the awareness. (John 14:27, Ephesians 4:17-19, 1Timothy 4:1-2)

Key Points About Self Image

I. **Understanding Pride (See Psalm 10:3-4, Romans 8:5-7, Acts 12:21-23, and Daniel 4:31-32)**
   A. Pride can be defined as a mind set on self with resistance to the will of God.
   B. A prideful person raises his standard for thinking, speaking and behaving above God's standard.
   C. A prideful person has a view of himself that is based on his opinions and ideals apart from the Truth of God's Word.

II. **Understanding Humility (See John 3:26-30, Romans 12:3, and Romans 8:5-7)**
   A. Humility is a mind set on Christ with submission to the will of God.
   B. Humility is embracing a view of one's self according to the standards of God not the opinions of man or his own views.
   C. A humble person adjusts his standards to align with will of God.

III. **Definition of Self Image**
   A. One's perspective of himself.
   B. One understands of who he is and who he is not.
   C. One's perspective of his role in life.

IV. **If one builds his self-image on the opinions of others, the culture and personal opinions he will develop an inaccurate self image.**
   A. It will lead the person to have an inaccurate assessment of their self before God (See Luke 18:9-14).
   B. This person will ultimately be trusting in mankind and his own flesh to understand himself which leads him away from Truth and from God (See Jeremiah 17:5-6).
   C. This person will be walking in earthly, natural, demonic wisdom (See James 3:13-16).

V. **If one builds his self-image on what God says is true about him according to Scripture he will develop an accurate self image.**
   A. It will be based on what God's Word says is true about himself (See John 8:31-32).
   B. This person ultimately will be trusting in Jesus Christ to explain who he is and who he is not (See John 8:31-32).
   C. This person will be walking in Heavenly, Spiritual, Godly wisdom (See Romans 12:2-3).

Key Points About Self Love

I. Understanding Love
- A. Eros—love that is based on erotic pleasure. The greater the pleasure one gets from the other person, the greater the love one has for that person; the lesser the pleasure one gets from that person the less love they have for that person; it is conditioned upon pleasure.
- B. Stergo—love that is conditioned upon the fact that we have kinship (ex. Brother, Cousin, Uncle etc.). Since we are family I treat you okay but if we were not family I would not have any dealings with you; it is conditioned upon family connection.
- C. Phileo—love that is based upon affection for the person according to some attraction to them, like interest, common goals or aspirations. The more attraction one feels, pleasure one has or common interest that is developed the more they love the other person; the less attraction one feels, the less pleasure one has with the other person or the less they have in common with the other person they loose love for the other person; it is conditioned upon attraction and common interest or pleasures.
- D. Agape—love that is based upon the power of God to seek the highest of good others unconditionally, no strings attached. "It is concerned not with how we feel but how we act. It responds not to the attractiveness of the other person but to the condition and need of the other person. Its motivation is not the selfish desire to enjoy the other person but the selfless desire to benefit him. Essentially, it is concerned and benevolent toward others."[13]

II. The love that God primarily commands is Agape love (See Matthew 22:34-40 and John 14:21).
- A. To love God is to keep His commandments as given in His Word.
- B. To love others is to seek the highest good of others and not to cause any harm to others.
- C. God does not command us to love ourselves.
- D. Self love is not something that has to be taught or commanded because it is something we already do on various levels.

---

[13]James Boyer, *For a World Like Ours: Studies in 1 Corinthians* (Grand Rapids, Michigan: Baker Book House, 1971).

III. Definition of Self Love
   A. Regard for one's self.
   B. Regard for one's own happiness.
   C. Regard for one's own advantage.

IV. The Scripture implies that we already love ourselves:
   A. Selfish Self Love—making self the priority for life; making self the central interest of existence (See 2Timohty 3-1-5).
   B. Self Preserving Self Love—the natural tendency to take care of ourselves and preserve our material bodies (See Ephesians 5:28-29).
   C. Soul-Loving Self Love—one's effort to gain wisdom and live accordingly in order guard and protect one's heart (See Proverb 19:8).

V. Scripture teaches that selfish self love leads to difficulty (See 2Timothy3:1-2).
   A. Preoccupation with self breeds selfishness (See James 3:13-4:7).
   B. Preoccupation with self breeds conflict with others (See James 3:13-4:7).
   C. Preoccupation with self produces disorder and every evil thing (See James 3:16).

VI. Scripture teaches us to deny selfish self love (See Luke 9:23-26).
   A. We are to focus on becoming like Christ in all aspects of life (See Ephesians 4:11-16).
   B. We are to focus on the Kingdom agenda of God (See Luke 12:13-48).
   C. We are no longer to live for ourselves but for Christ (See 2Corinthians 5:11-21).

The Premise of Self Image

Even though we are not to focus on improving our self-esteem, we are called to think soberly about ourselves (Self Image).

Definition of Self Image: One's perspective of himself; one's understanding of who he is, who he is not; one's perspective of his role in life

I. We are commanded to have a sober view of ourselves (See Romans 12:3).

  A. We are to have right thinking about ourselves (See Romans 12:3).
  B. We are to see ourselves according to God's Standard (See Ephesians 2:1-22).
  C. We must not view ourselves according to personal opinions (See Galatians 6:3).

II. We must view ourselves as created in the image of God (See Genesis 1:26-31).

  A. We were created to reflect God's character (See Genesis 1:26-31).
  B. We were created to be relational (See Genesis 2:18).
  C. We were created to be worshippers of God (See John 4:23-24).
  D. We have been designed with intellect (See Proverbs 23:7).
  E. We have been designed with a will (See Ecclesiastes 2:4-8).
  F. We have been designed with emotions (See Acts 20:36-38).

III. We must view ourselves according to our biological design (Genesis1:26-27).

  A. If we were created male we must view ourselves according to our male distinctions and functions (See 1Corinthians 11:1-12).
  B. If we were created female we must view ourselves according to our female distinctions and functions (See 1Corinthians 11:1-12).

IV. We must view ourselves according to our Position in Christ (See 2Corinthians 5:17).

  A. Man in Christ is forgiven of His sin against God (See 1John 2:1-2).
  B. Man in Christ is placed in the family of God (See Ephesians 2:11-19).
  C. Man in Christ is made alive from within to connect with God (See Ephesians 2:1-10).
  D. Man in Christ is given the Holy Spirit to empower him to live as God desires (See Romans 8:12-17).
  E. Man in Christ is set apart to God and made useful and pleasing to God through the power of the Holy Spirit working in him (See Ephesians 2:8-10).

V. We must view ourselves according to the Biblical Roles we have been given.
   A. Husband/Wife (See Ephesians 5:18-33, Colossians 3:18-19, and I Peter 3:1-12.)
   B. Son/Daughter (See Ephesians 6:1-2 and Colossians 3:20.)
   C. Parent (See Ephesians 6:4, Colossians 3:21, Deuteronomy 6:6-9, and Proverbs 22:6.)
   D. Friend (See Proverbs 27:5-6; 17:17; 27:9; and 18:24.)
   E. Leader (See I Timothy 4:16, Hebrews 13:7, 17; I Peter 5:5, I Timothy 5:17-22, and Luke 6:40.)
   F. Employer/Employee (See Ephesians 6:5-9 and I Peter 2:18-29.)

VII. We must view ourselves according to our Spiritual Giftedness (1Peter 4:10)
   A. We must see ourselves as servants with gifts to benefit the body (See 1Peter 4:10-11).
   B. We must know what our gifts are (See 1Corinthains 12:1-11).
   C. We must use our gifts accordingly (See Romans 12:3-8).

Key Point: *Self Esteem is a result not a pursuit. Therefore, Christians should be concentrating on loving God and others in the power of the Holy Sprit and not upon improving their "self esteem". As he loves consistently, the result will be positive self-esteem. As he is unloving the result will be negative self-esteem. Even though we are not to focus on improving our self-esteem we are called to think soberly about ourselves. This is where we understand the concept of Self Image. This differs from having dissatisfaction or satisfaction with ourselves (self-esteem). Self image is the evaluation of how one sees his role and position in life. Also we need to understand that loving self is an implied reality that fits in three categories. (Self-centered, Self Preserving, Soul loving) Once we understand the categories of self love we will have a better understanding of what it means to deny ourselves (See Romans 2:14-17, Proverbs 28:1, Genesis 4:6-7, Romans 12:3, and Ephesians 5:28-29.)*

Section Eleven

Thinking Affects the Body

I. Key Point: *The way we think affects our body. Scripture asserts that the thoughts which one chooses to entertain in his heart—those for which he is said to be responsible to God—can either help or hinder the health of his physical body.*

    A. Rejoicing and obedience in the Lord helps us to overcome the hard times in life (See Proverbs 17:22; 3:5-8; 4:20-22; 14:30).

    B. A broken spirit hurts a person physiologically in body and brain. (See Proverbs 17:22).

    C. Guilt and fear can produce bodily feelings and responses as your immaterial heart interacts with your material brain and body (See Psalm 32:1-4, Psalm 38:1-10, 18, and 1Corinthians 11:30).

    D. How does a ringing of a bell bring on an asthma attack?

        1. Bell rings > person relives rejection< unloving attitudes occur > guilt >fear > asthma* *Fear of judgment (fear with not apparent cause) in the immaterial heart triggers a reaction in the brain and body, which results in an asthma attack

(Insights adapted from <u>The Heart of Man and The Mental Disorders</u> by Rich Thomson)

Two Level Sin Issues

II. Key Point: *A two level sin is a sin that is used to flee from one's sense of guilt and fear of judgment regarding sin. This makes it a two level sin.*

    A. Drunkenness (alcoholism) and drug abuse are examples of two-level sin issues. One is fleeing the anxiety, guilt of some other sin by drinking or doing drugs. Drinking and doing drugs is an escape from the root sin but they themselves are sinful practices thus making it a two-level sin issue (See Galatians 5:20-21, Proverbs 20:1 and Romans 13:13).

    B. Some sexual disorders are examples of two-level sin issues. Compulsive pornography is a form of fleeing. It helps a person numb fear and guilt in his heart from some other sin (See Galatians 5:19, Matthew 5:28). Nymphomania (woman who has different men sex partners all the time) and Satyriasis (man who has different women sex partners all the time are forms of fleeing. It helps the person feel good and relax in order to numb fear and guilt in his/her heart from some other sin (See 1Thessalonians 4:3-8, 1Corinthians 6:18-20). Homosexuality is a form of fleeing. They have exchanged what they are designed for and moved away from it to that which they were not designed for. They are fleeing from their unloving attitudes towards the opposite sex. They are fleeing from hetero-sexual relationship issues (See Leviticus 18:22, 20:13, 1Corinthians 6:9, 1Timothy 1:10, Genesis 19:4-11, Judges 19:22-25, and Romans 1:26-27).

C. Some manias like kleptomania (compulsive stealing) and pyromania (setting of fires) are examples of two-level sins. These persons may steal or set fire to flee from the guilt and fear of some root sin (See Ephesians 4:28 and Romans 12:17b; 13:9-10).

D. Suicide is an example of a two-level sin. In order to escape the guilt and fear of some sin(s) one seeks to kill himself (See Matthew 27:3-5).

E. False religion is an example of a two-level sin. In order to clear one's conscience of guilt and fear one flees to false religion resulting in a peace that the world gives instead of coming to Christ (See Romans 1:23, Deuteronomy 12:30-31, Jeremiah 10:2-5, Colossians 2:23, and 1 Timothy 4:1-3).

(Insights adapted from The Heart of Man and The Mental Disorders by Rich Thomson)

Hypercriticism /Personality Conflict

III. Key Point: *Two people are likely to be hypercritical of one another or have personality conflicts even when there is no specific issue between them because they are seeing their own sin in another person. A person may flee paying attention to his own sin by being hypercritical (intolerantly critical) of another person for the same sin for which he himself is guilty (at least guilty in the heart). This is more properly understood as detection and rejection rather than projection. One detects his own weakness in another and is intolerant of it to the degree to which he excuses it in his own life (See Matthew 7:1-5, Romans 2:1-3, and 2 Samuel 12:1-7).*

    A. Generally, this results in people detecting their sin in another person and rejecting that person according to that sin instead of dealing with that sin in their own life (See Romans 2:1-3).

    B. When you find that you can't have peace in a circumstance until a person changes some attitude, word or action you may be detecting something in them that you have not been paying attention to in yourself (See Matthew 7:1-5).

    C. The more bothered you are about another's sin (where you are unloving in thoughts, words, or actions or lack peace) the more you may be detecting something that you have not been dealing with in your life (See 2 Samuel 12:1-7).

D. This helps us understand why some relationships in a family are more difficult than others. There is hypercriticism involved in the lives of both parties. Likewise, this helps us understand why some relationships in any group are more difficult than others. Those persons which we find hard to love may be exposing areas of our lives that are hard for us to face in ourselves. Knowing what particularly gripes us about someone else helps us to understand the weaknesses we have in our own heart (See 2 Samuel 12:1-7, Matthew 7:1-5, and Romans 2:1-3).

E. This principle helps us understand why (all other things being equal) one child in the family is rebellious while other children in the same family are not. That one child may strongly exhibit the same weakness as one of the parents and be rejected hypercritically by that parent, thus fomenting rebellion (See 2 Samuel 12:1-7, Matthew 7:1-5, and Romans 2:1-3).

F. This principle may also help us to understand why biblical counselors can tend more critical of some people whom they counsel than of others.

Insights adapted from The Heart of Man and The Mental Disorders by Rich Thomson

Expressions and Their Root Cause

Using the expression sheet and framework you have learned in this study:

A. Identify which expression best fits under uncaused fear

B. Identify which expression best fits under uncaused fleeing

C. Identify the root cause of these expressions

D. Place your answers on the chart below

Indecisiveness, rebellion, lack of confidence, shunning responsibility, depression, avoiding coming home, anxiousness, having an affair, panicky, workaholic, blame shifting, drug abuse, over accommodation, fidgety, alcoholism, withdrawing, restlessness, unwilling to expose ideas, overly aware of self, putting on a façade, living in the shadows of others, pornography, homosexuality, hesitating to be honest, overly sensitive to criticism, defensive, withdrawing and refusing to talk to each other, tense, panic attacks, multiple personalities, schizophrenia

Root Cause   **Uncaused Fear**   **Uncaused Fleeing**

Biblical Diagnosis

Review this case and using the form on the next page seek to identify and write down :

    A. expressions of uncaused fleeing (if there are any)

    B. expressions of uncaused fear (if there are any)

    C. expressions of a sense of guilt (if there are any)

    D. secondary unloving attitudes, words or actions (if there are any)

Case Study

Kenneth is a 45 year old male. Yesterday he was told by his boss that the company would be downsizing and would no longer need his services. Kenneth was not shaken he politely asked when his last day would be and kindly walked out of the office. Over the last few weeks Kenneth has been experiencing many panic attacks on his way to work. His friends report that Kenneth has been eating more than usual, oversleeping and coming in late to work. Kenneth told his friends that the boss has put a camera in Kenneth's house and is watching his every move. Kenneth also believes that his boss has hired hit men to come after him. Kenneth is scared to go outside because he believes his boss is following him. He has been calling in sick and finding reasons why he cannot leave his home. Kenneth has gained about ten pounds in the last five weeks and is refusing to take a bath or clean himself up. Kenneth tries to find every excuse possible not to communicate with his boss.

Evaluating a Counseling Problem or Mental Disorder from the Word

Using the Biblical Framework put the defining features of the problem in the category that best fit.

1. Defining features which are expressions of apparently uncaused fleeing

2. Defining features which are expressions of apparently uncaused fear.

3. Defining features which are expressions of knowledge and/or a sense of guilt.

4. Defining features which are expression of unloving attitudes, words, and or actions (Secondary unloving expressions).

5. Physiological defining features which are so consistently present with the above defining features that they should be understood as physiological results in one's body or brain of apparently uncaused fear or a sense of guilt

(Sheet developed by Rich Thomson)

Section Twelve
Forgiveness

Key Point: *The more one counts on the fact of how forgiven he is, the greater and deeper his forgiveness will be for others. Once we see how wretched we are and how much we are forgiven the more we are inclined to forgive others. However we must not confuse forgiving people with loving people (See Ephesians 4:32, Luke 17:3-4, Mattew 18:15-18, 21-35, 1John 1:9, Psalm 32:1-5, and Galatians 6:1-2.)*

Definition of Forgiveness: To disregard, to let go of, to release from, to pardon, and to cancel a debt owed

I. Here is what we must consider about Sin and Forgiveness: (Romans 5:6-11)
   A. Forgiveness of sin is possible because of the sacrifice of Jesus Christ; He paid the penalty for our sins. He made the sacrifice of His life for the saving of ours from the penalty of sin (See Romans 5:6-11, Romans 6:23, 1John 2:1-2).
   B. Forgiveness of sin results in the judicial act of one being made legally right with God forever; His sins no longer count against him as it relates to damnation. God is no longer angry with him. He is reconciled to a right relationship with God—Judicial Forgiveness/Reconciliation (See Romans 5:1, 6-11).
   C. Once one is judicially set free from the penalty of sin He still has to deal with God in His daily actions of sin which hinder his fellowship with God. Until he confesses and repents of this sin in his daily life he is unable to walk in fellowship with God and walk in love towards others since he is in the flesh. When confession and repentance takes place forgiveness of sin takes place resulting in restoration of proper fellowship with God—Parental Forgiveness (See 1John 1:9, Matthew 18:21-35, Proverbs 28:13, and Psalm 32:3-5).
   D. Since Jesus paid the penalty for all sins committed by mankind the penalty for sin has been satisfied through Him; If one refuses to accept Christ's payment for sin they will not receive forgiveness of their sin and have to pay for their own sin (See 1John 2:1-2, John 3:16-18, and Romans 6:23).

II. Here are the implications of Sin and Forgiveness (Ephesians 4:32)
   A. Forgiveness of sin is available to all but not granted until one deals with his sin accordingly (See Psalm 32:1-5, 1John 3: 8-12, Matthew 6:14-15, and Luke 15:11-32).
   B. God loves unconditionally but He grants forgiveness of sin on the basis of confession and repentance (See Romans 5:8, Proverbs 28:13, Psalm 32:1-5, and James 5:16).
   C. We can love others unconditionally but we cannot grant forgiveness of sin to others until the sin is confessed and repented of (See Luke 6:27-36, Romans 12:9-21, and Matthew 18:15-17).
   D. Sin must be confronted, confessed, and repented of before it is forgiven (See Galatians 6:1-2, Matthew 18:15-17, and 2Samuel 12:1-15).

(Based upon the insights above we can clearly see the application of Luke 17:1-4)

III. Sin Issues are inevitable therefore we need to be on Guard (v1-v3)
   A. You cannot avoid people trying to lead you into sin or sinning against you.
   B. It would be bad for you if you are the stumbling block to others in this way since it will bring negative consequences to your life.
   C. We need to watch ourselves and help keep others from becoming a stumbling block.
   D. We need to identify where we are stumbling blocks and help others identify where they are a stumbling blocks.

IV. We need to deal with Sin Issues and Forgiveness Accordingly (v3-v4)
   A. We must confront clear sin lovingly before it can be forgiven.
   B. If clear sin is confessed and repented of it can then be forgiven.
   C. As long as the sin is confessed and repented of it does not matter how often it happens it must be forgiven accordingly and put up with patiently.
   D. If there is no confession and repentance of the sin there can be no forgiveness of the sin. The sin issue must then be taken before witnesses and ultimately before the Church leadership if not confessed and repented of before witnesses.

Ten Step Guide to Dealing with Sin and Forgiveness

1. Before one confronts another about an issue he must determine if it is a personal preference issue, expectation issue or clear sin before approaching the person (See Proverbs 13:3).

2. If it is a personal preference issue or expectation issue confrontation may not need to happen because no sin has occurred; only disappointment and denial of a particular desire. Dealing with preferences and expectations is the issue. This needs to be considered personally to determine if it even needs to be addressed since it is not a sin issue (See Romans 14:1-22).

3. One must identify all unloving thoughts, words, and actions within self in response to the preference issue, expectation issue or clear sin. and confess and repent of all unloving thoughts, words, and actions to God and to others when appropriate (See Proverbs 28:13).

4. After dealing with self one must confront the person about clear sin with the intent to restore them not with the intent to destroy them (See Luke 17:3-4, Galatians 6:1-2, Proverbs 27:6a, and 1Thessalonians 5:15).

5. If the person confesses and repents of the sin forgive them (See Luke 17:3-4).

6. If the person confesses and repents of the sin dismiss it and never bring it up again (See Luke 17:3 and 1Peter 4:8).

7. If the person refuses to confess and repent of the sin bring witnesses to address it (See Matthew 18:15-17).

8. If the person refuses to confess and repent of the sin with witnesses take it to the leadership of the Church so that they can address it (See Matthew 18:15-17).

9. No matter what the reaction of the other person or the outcome of the situation one should be an open channel of love to the person (See Luke 6:27-36).

10. One should pray and do well to the person (See Luke 6:27-36, Romans 12:14, 20-21, and 1Peter 3:9).

Section Thirteen
Decision Making In the Will of God

I. Key Point: *We must learn to make good, Godly decisions. In order to do this we must categorize between moral and non-moral issues. Moral issues are spelled out in the bible. These issues are stated as either right or wrong in the Word of God. With these issues you only have to decide if you will or will not obey. Non-moral issues are issues that the bible does not classify as either right or wrong. You have freedom to decide the path you will take. However, the choice must be made in faith or the person is sinning. (Romans 14:22-23) When making decisions on non-moral issues one has to use wisdom and not allow his freedom to choose become a license to sin (See Romans 14 and James 4:17).*

    A. Some decisions are clearly stated as right and wrong in Scripture. One should decide to obey God's Word by faith (See John 14:15).

    B. Some decisions are made by one's biblically ordained authority. The biblically ordained authorities are husbands, parents, employers, church leaders, and government. You must comply with their decisions within the parameters of their God-given authority. Therefore, God's will in those situations is that you follow the orders of the authority within the parameters given by God (See Ephesians 5:22-6:9, Colossians 3:18-4:1, Titus 2:5-3:2, Hebrews 13:17, 1 Peter 2:13-3:7, and Romans 13:1-7).

        1. One should submit even if the decisions seem unreasonable or a matter of preference (See Ephesians 5:24 and 1Peter 2:18-20).

        2. One should submit to the decisions while communicating openly in love (See Proverbs 27:6a).

        3. One should submit to decisions without attempting to manipulate authority. Here are some examples:

Open and Unloving Ways	*Closed and Unloving Ways*
1. Verbal Anger	1. Physical Withdrawal
2. Temper Tantrum	2. Silence
3. Physical Violence	3. Flattery
4. Making a Public Scene	4. Pouting
5. Nagging	5. Uncooperative
6. Begging	6. Talking behind back
7. Shaming	7. Sighing
8. Criticizing	8. Slowing down/stop helping
9. Threatening	9. Looking sad
10. Bribing	10. Insincere favors or gifts
11. Whining	
12. Crying	
13. Going on Strike	

C. One should not submit to the decisions if they are in direct violation of the Word of God. Even then one should try to give a biblical alternative before respectfully declining to submit. If necessary, accepting to suffer for righteousness' sake (See Acts 4:19; 5:29, Daniel 1:8-13, 1 Peter 3:13-17, and 4:12-19).

D. Where the bible does not categorize an issue as right or wrong you have the freedom to choose preferentially. These are issues that we categorize as non-moral. These issues have no moral implications; the choice is based upon your preference (See Romans 14: 1-23 and 1Corinthians 8:1-13).

E. Although you may have freedom to choose preferentially in issues that are categorized as non-moral, do not allow you freedom to become a license to sin against God by allowing that which you have chosen to lead you into sin. Let your freedom of choice be used as a license to serve God by allowing that which you have chosen to lead you into holy living, i.e. entertainment, food, job, ministry service, husband, wife, church worship (See 1Corinthians 6:12-20, 1Peter 2:16, Romans 14:13-21, and 1Corinthians 8:4-13).

F. These decisions should be made by using biblical principles like the following:
1. One should make sure that he is controlled by the Holy Spirit (See Psalm 66:18, 1 John 1:9, Proverbs 28:13, Ephesians 5:18, and Galatians 5:16).
2. One should identify any and all biblical principles that may apply to the issue (See Romans 12:2, 2Timothy 3:16-17, Psalm 1:1-3, and Proverbs 19:2-3).
3. One should seek to gather as much relevant data as possible—i.e. books, magazines, articles, website info etc. (See Proverbs 14:8, 15, 16).
4. One should seek wisdom from persons who are knowledgeable in that area in which they are seeking to make decisions. One should get counsel and information. One should not seek to get the person to make a decision for them. (See Proverbs 11:14, Proverbs 20:5, Proverbs 19:20, and Proverbs 15:22).
5. Once should weigh the pros and cons of his alternatives and then make a decision according to the alternative that seems to have more pro's than con's (See Proverbs 14:15-16).
6. He must accept by faith that he has not sinned in his choice. He must accept the consequences that come with the choice (See Proverbs 16:1, 9).
7. He must accept that God will either allow it to go forward as chosen or God may re-direct as He sees fit—we choose God decides (See Proverbs 16: 1, 9 and James 4:13-17).

(Insights adapted from Rich Thomson)

Decision Making Exercise

1. Identify the issue or issues whereby you have to make a decision.

2. Determine if the issue is a moral or non-moral issue.

3. Determine if the issue is to be addressed by those who are in authority over you.

4. Research the Scripture to see what it has to say on the issue both directly and indirectly. Write down what you find.

5. Research any and all forms of information to gather relevant data on the issues. Write down what you find.

6. Talk with people who have expertise on these issues and write down what you find.

7. Identify the pros and cons of each alternative and write down what you find.

8. Make a decision in faith. Write down your decision and explain why you chose that alternative instead the other alternatives.

Section Fourteen

Distinguishing Between Sharing and Gossiping

I. If we are going to develop in effective communication we need to learn the danger of being careless with our words when talking about other people. Carelessness in our words can lead to speaking lies about someone unintentionally and sometimes intentionally. (Proverbs 12:22, 15:7, 28)

   A. When you do not speak the truth you tend to give *__misinformation-__* presenting information about something or someone that is partially the truth or information that is completely wrong.

   B. When you do not speak the truth you tend to give *__misrepresentations-__* presenting information about something or someone it as if it were true; not presenting them properly, carefully or truthfully.

   C. When you do not speak the truth you tend to give *__exaggerations-__* presenting information about something or someone by describing something larger, better, or worse than it really is.

   D. When you do not speak the truth you tend to make *__allegations-__* making unfounded assertions; implying something is fact without proof.

(Adapted from the book Friendly Fire by Jim Morris)

II. Before we begin to have a discussion about a person there are some factors that need be considered. (Proverbs 10:14, 19, 11:13)

   A. We need to guard our *__tongues__* so that we do not bring unnecessary trouble to our lives as a result of the words spoken about another person that should not have been said from the beginning. (Proverbs 21:23, 18:6-7)

   B. We need to make sure that we are communicating what is *__appropriate__* when speaking about another person. (Proverbs 10:32)

C. We need to make sure that we are communicating what is ***helpful*** not ***hurtful*** when speaking about another person. (Proverbs 16:24)

D. In essence, we need to restrain ourselves from saying ***too*** much about a person and from speaking ***mess*** or ***garbage*** about a person. (Proverbs 12:23)

III. Before we begin to have a discussion about someone, we need to determine if we are about to gossip. (Proverbs 20:19, 10:18, 16:28, 26:20-22)

A. Gossip is when information about another individual or set of individuals is shared that is supposed to be kept ***confidential***.(Proverbs 20:19)

B. Gossip is when negative or confidential information about another individual or set of individuals whether true or false is shared about them, not to them, with the intent to put down, ***criticize***, embarrass, ruin reputations, or bring unwarranted/ unproven accusations against the person. (Proverbs 10:18)

C. Gossip is when negative or confidential information about another individual or set of individuals whether true or false is shared about them, not to them, with the intent to bring unwarranted ***division*** between people. (Proverbs 16:28)

D. Gossip is when negative or confidential information about another individual or set of individuals whether true or false is shared about them, not to them, with intent to create ***mess*** and ***conflict*** between people. (Proverbs 26:20-22)

IV. It is not considered gossip when negative or confidential information that is proven to be true is shared with the proper leadership in order for that leadership to do what is right as prescribed by God in His Word to bring order, peace, reconciliation, church discipline or whatever is needed to the Glory of God, the good of the individual(s) involved and the good of the church.

A. Sharing the faults of others is permitted when proven credible facts/ truth, not perceptions or preferences whether negative or confidential about another individual or set of individuals is reported to ***leadership*** in relation to ***unresolved disunity*** among the brethren within the congregation so that leadership can address it biblically. (Philippians 4:2-3)

B. Sharing the faults of others is permitted when proven credible facts/truth, not perceptions or preferences, whether negative or confidential about another individual or a set of individuals is reported to ***leadership*** in relation to ***unrepentant sexual immorality*** within the congregation so that leadership can address it biblically. (1Corinthians 5:1-3)

C. Sharing the faults of others is permitted when proven credible facts/truth not perceptions or preferences, whether negative or confidential about another individual or a set of individuals is reported to ***leadership*** in relation to ***division being spread*** among the congregation so that leadership can address it biblically. (1Corinthians 1:10-11)

D. Sharing the faults others is permitted when proven credible facts/truth not perceptions or preferences, whether negative or confidential about another individual or a set of individuals is reported to ***leadership*** in relation to ***unrepentant sin*** so that leadership can address it biblically. (Matthew 18:15-17)

V. What are some ways I can talk to someone about my problem with someone else, without gossiping or condemning the person with whom I have a problem?

    A. Share your concerns with wise counsel without being ***malicious*** towards the person with whom you have the problem. (1Peter 3:8-12)

    B. Share your concerns with wise counsel without ***vilifying*** the person with whom you have a problem but seeking to gain knowledge in the matter. (Proverbs 11:9)

    C. Share your concerns with wise counsel without making yourself the ***hero*** or the ***victim*** in the matter knowing that there is always two sides to every story. (Proverbs 18:17, 10:32)

    D. Share your concerns with wise counsel with the intent of learning how to be at ***peace*** with others. (Romans 12:17-18)

    E. Share your concerns with wise counsel with the intent of learning what you can do to ***change yourself*** within your role and responsibility, instead of sharing your concerns with the intent of trying to figure out what you can do to fix or change the other person. (Matthew 7:1-5)

What Should We Do When Al talks negatively to Betty about Carl?
(See Ephesians 4:29)

A. <u>**If You are Al You Should:**</u>

1. Confess your unloving attitude and action to God as sin. Approach Carl about Carl's fault at the appropriate time (See 1 John 1:9 and Proverbs 27:6).

2. At the appropriate time acknowledge your wrong to Betty for having spoken of Carl's fault—and even share that you have spoken to Carl about it without giving the details of the conversation (See James 5:16).

B. <u>***If You are Betty You Should:***</u>

1. At the appropriate time encourage Al to speak to Carl while you give Carl the benefit of the doubt (See Ephesians 4:15 and 1 Corinthians 13:7).

2. Not mention the conversation to Carl because in so doing you will be talking about Al behind Al's back and exposing Al's sin at the same time (See Proverbs 17:9).

3. Give Al a time frame by which he should speak with Carl and hold him accountable to do it (See Hebrews 3:12-13, 10:24 and Galatians 6:1-2).

C. <u>**If You are Carl You Should:**</u>

1. Speak with Al to resolve the matter (See Matthew 5:23-24).

2. As much as it depends on you seek peace with Al (See Romans 12:18).

3. Bring in others into the matter if it cannot be resolved with you and Al (See Matthew 18:15-21 and Proverbs 17:9).

D. The Process to Practice: How does this Apply in a Counseling Situation? (See Proverbs 18:15, 17, Luke 17:3-4, Proverbs 20:5, Galatians 6:1-2.)

1. Remember to counsel the person who is there not the person who is not there. That is, your counsel should be directed at helping the person who is in your presence not the person who hurt him. You do not have all the details because the other person is not there (See Proverbs 18:15, 17 and Ephesians 4:29).

2. Stop the counselee from talking about or exposing the character flaws of the person that hurt them because that person is not there to defend their point of view (See Luke 17:3-4 and Proverbs 18:17).

3. Ask the counselee if they have discussed this issue with the person that has hurt them (See Matthew 18:15-17 and Proverbs 27:6).

4. Help the counselee determine if the hurt was based on a personal preference issue, expectation issue or clear sin issue that has taken place against them by the other person (See Proverbs 20:5).

5. If it is determined that the counselee is dealing with a personal preference issue or expectation issue help them to take responsibility for their own feelings, desires, expectations, disappointments in the matter. Help them to identify how they are reacting in thoughts, words, actions, or relationship patterns to the one that has hurt them. Help the counselee to identify, confess and repent of all unloving, thoughts, words, and actions in response to the hurt (See Proverbs 20:5, Proverbs 28:13, and Galatians 6:1-2).

6. If it is determined that the counselee is dealing with a clear sin issue help them to take responsibility for their own feelings, desires, expectations, disappointments in the matter. Help the counselee to identify how he is reacting in thoughts, words, actions, or relationship patterns to the one that has sinned against him. Help the counselee to identify, confess and repent of all unloving, thoughts, words, and actions in response to the hurt (See Proverbs 20:5, Proverbs 28:13, and Galatians 6:1-2).

7. In either case help the counselee focus on thanking God for the grief, pain, and disappointment God has allowed knowing God will use it to build him up (See James 1:1-8, 1Thessalonians 5:18, and Romans 5:1-5).

8. Help the counselee identify how he consistently relates to those with whom he is having the most difficulty. Help him identify his loving and unloving patterns of relating (See1Coritnthians 13:4-7).

9. If it is determined that the counselee is dealing with a personal preference issue or expectation issue instruct the counselee to go to that person and share their grief as a result of the hurt ,if sharing will be helpful and not an avenue for manipulation (See Ephesians 4:29).

10. If it is determined that the counselee is dealing with a clear sin, the counselee must be instructed to confront the person about clear sin with the intent to restore them not with the intent to destroy them (See Luke 17:3-4, Galatians 6:1-2, Proverbs 27:6a, and 1Thessalonians 5:15).

11. The counselor must explain to the counselee that:
    a. If the person confesses and repents of the sin forgive them (See Luke 17:3-4).
    b. If the person confesses and repents of the sin, dismiss it and never bring it up again (See Luke 17:3, 1Peter 4:8).
    c. If the person refuses to confess and repent of the sin bring witnesses to address it (See Matthew 18:15-17).
    d. If the person refuses to confess and repent of the sin with witnesses take it to the leadership of the Church so that they can address it (See Matthew 18:15-17).
    e. No matter what the reaction of the other person or the outcome of the situation one should be an open channel of love to the person; one should pray and do good to the person (See Luke 6:27-36, Romans 12:14,20-21, and 1Peter 3:9).

   (Insights adapted from Rich Thomson)

Bibliography

Adams, Jay. How to Help People Change, Grand Rapids: Zondervan, 1986.

Adams, Jay Solving Marriage Problems, Grand Rapids: Zondervan, 1983.

Berg, Jim. Changed into His Image: God's Plan for Transforming Your Life, Greenville, SC: Bob Jones University Press, 2000.

Colson, Charles. How Now Shall We Live, Wheaton: Tyndale House Publishing, Inc., 1999.

Fitzpatrick, Elyse. Idols of the Heart, Phillipsburg: P & R Publishing Company, 2001.

Jamieson, Robert, A. R. Fausset, and David Brown, A Commentary: Critical, Experimental, and Practical on the Old and New Testament. 3 vols. Rpt., Grand Rapids: Wm. Eerdman's Publishing, 1978.

Hendriksen, William, New Testament Commentary: Exposition of Thessalonians, Timothy, and Titus, Grand Rapids: Baker Book House, 1973.

Lenski, R.C.H., The Interpretation of Matthew's Gospel, Minneapolis: Augsburg Publishing House, 1946.

Kittel, Gerhard, ed., Theological Dictionary of the New Testament, Vols. 1-4, Grand Rapids: Wm. B. Eerdman's Publishing Co., 1964.

Mounce, William D. The Analytical Lexicon to the Greek New Testament, Grand Rapids: Zondervan Publishing House, 1993.

Noebel, David. Thinking like a Christian (Teaching Textbook) Nashville: Broadman–Holman Publishers, 2002.

Piper, John. God's Passion for His Glory, Wheaton Illinois: Crossway Books 1998

Rienecker, Fritz and Cleon L. Rogers, eds. Linguistic Key to the Greek New Testament, Grand Rapids: Zondervan Corporation, 1976.

Scott, Stuart The Exemplary Husband: A Biblical Perspective, Bemidiji, MN: Focus Publishing, 2000.

Thomson, Rich. The Heart of Man and The Mental Disorders, Houston: Biblical Counseling Ministries, Inc., 2004.

Tripp, Paul David. Instruments in the Redeemer's Hands, People in Need of Change Helping People in Need of Change, Phillipsburg, NJ: P&R Publ., 2002.

www.ingramcontent.com/pod-product-compliance
Lightning Source LLC
Chambersburg PA
CBHW080553230426

43663CB00015B/2816